AFTER THE FALKLANDS

Finally Overcoming the Nightmare of PTSD

AFTER THE FALKLANDS
Finally Overcoming the Nightmare of PTSD

Cover Photography Copyright: **Imperial War Museum**
Book Cover Design by **Andy Grey** (Andy@andygrey.co.uk) and
Wendy Dashwood-Quick (wendy@resolutioncoaching.co.uk)
Book Typesetting by **Neil Coe** neil@cartadesign.co.uk

Set in **Adobe Garamond** 11 on 14pt

First published in 2007 by;

Ecademy Press
6 Woodland Rise, Penryn,
Cornwall UK TR10 8QD
info@ecademy-press.com
www.ecademy-press.com

Printed and Bound by;
Lightning Source in the UK and USA

Printed on acid-free paper from managed forests. This book is printed on demand, so no copies will be remaindered or pulped.

ISBN-978-1-905823-18-5

A CIP catalogue record for this book is available from the British Library.

WARNING

This book has been written about and with the assistance of veterans who have experienced the true horror of war. Our intention is to tell a story which many feel needs to be told – the story of real people returning from war and attempting to adjust to peacetime living. And the pain and suffering the veteran and their families experience when they develop PTSD as a consequences of serving their country.

Sometime the images are graphic and disturbing – war is like that, sometimes the language is coarse and direct – soldiers are like that and sometimes the stories can re-ignite old, deeply suppressed pain and dread in the mind of a veteran – PTSD is like that.

So if you are a veteran, or serving in the forces, and reading this book triggers anxiety, shame, grief or guilt – put the book down. There's no point battling on, causing yourself pain. Just put the book down and try and regain your composure. If this is difficult to do, if the memories are too intense, the feelings too real and sense of guilt and shame too overwhelming, you may be experiencing some symptoms of PTSD. Do try and tough it out. Seek help straight away and if you don't know where to turn, don't hesitate to contact us (PTSD@helpmeovercome.com or 0800 093 8571) and we'll do what we can get you the appropriate help you need.

Finally, these stories are about Falklands veterans who have gone through real physical and emotional trauma. To protect them and their family's name, places and times have been changed. If you do recognise an individual in these stories, please leave them in peace. They went to the darkest recesses of their soul to share with us. Please don't take them back there again – there is no need for them to relive their pain again.

ACKNOWLEDGEMENTS

There are so many people who have helped bring this book to life it is difficult to know where to begin.

Firstly I would like to thank the contributing authors Dr Robin Short and Martin Kinsella whose efforts have given a depth to this book that I would not have achieved alone. I would also like to take this opportunity to thank Jimmy Johnson for giving us permission to use the chapter "The Veteran Returns Home" from his book about PTSD. I sincerely hope that this will create a much higher level of awareness for Jimmy and the thousands of others in his situation so that one day justice can be done.

I would also like to thank the veterans and PTSD casualties who have given us permission to use their stories to highlight the plight of our ex-servicemen as they struggle, with minimal effective support in their private battles against PTSD.

I would like to thank Mindy (www.bookmidwife.com) without whom this book would just be another vague idea cluttering up my brain; and Andy of Ecademy Press who has worked so hard to bring this book to print in time for the climax of the Falklands commemorations. Also I would like to give Wendy (wendy@resolutioncoaching.co.uk) a massive vote of thanks for volunteering to provide the artwork and cover for this book. And to Terry Sako (sako@netnitco.net) USMC (Retd) for permission to use his poem PTSD–One.

I would like to take this opportunity to extend my heartfelt thanks to all my friends, colleagues and social networkers at Ecademy (www.ecademy.com) who have provided so much moral, emotional, technical and operational support to move this project to the place that it is today. This applies especially to all the members of the Falklands Campaign 2007 club on Ecademy, who have been so supportive and helpful in bringing this project together.

I would like to thank all those businesses and individuals who have offered support in the form of personal contributions and gift vouchers for the special rewards pack which is available to everyone who purchases this book. Please show your support to these people by visiting www.AfterTheFalklands.com and even if you don't need the product or service they are offering, please just send them a quick note to express your thanks for their social responsibility and sense of corporate charity.

Finally, I would like to thank all the service men and women who everyday put on the uniform of our Armed Forces to serve our country and strive to preserve the peace and freedom we have become so accustomed to in this great country we call home.

This book is dedicated to all our veterans who came home in body but not in mind.

CONTENTS

AFTER THE FALKLANDS

Finally Overcoming the Nightmare of PTSD

CHAPTER 1

RECOLLECTIONS

By
Dr. Robin Short

3 April 1982 - a defining moment in many lives. The surrender of the Falkland Islands to the invading Argentine Forces.

The resulting nationalistic fervour, the jingoism, the frenetic preparations by both Service and Civilian agencies to send an Invasion Force to recapture the Islands is still a vivid memory.

So is the long sea voyage with the preparations for the unthinkable. Then the recapture of South Georgia. The bombing of the airfield by a Vulcan bomber. The sinking of the Belgrano. The sinking of HMS Sheffield, Coventry and the Atlantic Conveyor. The anxious time during the landing at San Carlos and the loss of so many capital ships to Argentine aircraft attacks. The "yomp" across the Island, Goose Green and the subsequent decorations for valour tinged with loss due to bravery. The horrors of Bluff Cove. The battle for Mount Longdon and the surrender after Tumbledown and Wireless Ridge had been taken. The "Red and Green Life Machine" that saved so many. The demoralised and defeated Argentine Forces and their repatriation. All played out in front of the press, so all could see the horrors of modern warfare. The triumphant return by Canberra to a rapturous welcome. The subsequent parade and service in Westminster Abbey. Those are the public memories being revisited and revived twenty five years on, reinforcing and reminding us of the event.

This book details the experiences of a chosen few of those who gave for the Falklands and who subsequently suffered and lost their personal battle in life. These were the very best, bright young men who, judging from their service photographs, deteriorated after the conflict to become a shadow of their former persona. These are their stories.

There are those who have their personal anniversary every year and who dread its recurrence. Those for whom it all became too much to cope with and who took their own life to escape, more now than killed in the conflict. This is the true legacy of the Falklands conflict and of all conflicts before and since: Korea, Aden, Borneo, Bosnia, the Kuwait liberation and increasingly now in Iraq and Afghanistan. These casualties are predominantly Army, but also in the two other Services and now increasingly in the Territorial Army. Similarly, the Argentine soldiers appear to have considerable problems and a high suicide rate from correspondence with some involved.

I was in command of an Armoured Field Ambulance in Germany, dedicated to providing medical support to an Armoured Division in BAOR during the Falklands campaign. All my "medics" volunteered to go to join the conflict and had to be reminded of their primary task, which continued. There was considerable frustration felt by many to be left out. This was tempered two years later when we received an influx, most unusually, of medics from the Parachute Field ambulance and the Parachute Regiments. It very soon became apparent, when aircraft flew over the unit location or on exercise that many of these Falklands veterans had residual problems, which coupled with an increasing number of family and social problems, indicated that many had early signs of PTSD. The unit attempted internally to deal with these with education and support and had some success.

Thereafter I was aware that PTSD would be a problem in the aftermath of any conflict and psychiatric cover was included in the operational planning for the Gulf and was increased in Bosnia. In the Defence Medical Services Directorate a Staff Paper was prepared proposing methods to reduce the potential for PTSD and for review and treatment in the Services. Only the Royal Navy made progress at RNH Haslar and later in the Royal Marines. There was little recognition in the Army and no survey of units that had been in combat, even though it was suspected that there were those taking their discharge rather than admit their increasing disability.

The Peace Dividend and the Government Defence Studies programme closed the military hospitals and reduced the numbers in the Medical Services, especially the Psychiatric cadre. Eventually the last psychiatric facility closed. Military Wings at civilian hospitals took their place. The medical support for the Regular Forces had become reduced to levels which were, and are still, struggling to support current operational involvement. Our medical personnel are very experienced, very well trained, upholding the traditions, but too few for the tasks in hand.

I left the service having been Director General of the Army Medical Services.

My civilian employment thereafter was in Nursing and Residential Home management. One of the homes was uniquely dedicated to the treatment of ex-servicemen and women and Emergency Service Personnel who had PTSD. This gave me access to the clinics and the records of those who were attending, throughout the country. I also started from scratch a complete administrative record of those involved and was also able to study the treatments afforded. The task was to seek PCT funding for treatment. This was invariably unsuccessful even though there were no facilities available under the NHS to provide treatment, experience of late onset PTSD was very limited and provision of CPN support was very variable. Over six years this amounted to some 1500 personnel and over 500 treated by inpatient care. Sadly the facility had to close due to lack of funding. The loss was felt acutely by those who were involved and also those veteran PTSD casualties who depended upon it.

The picture emerged of discharge from the Services, success in transfer to civilian life. This was followed at a variable interval, perhaps triggered by some event, by a descent into excess drinking, family breakdown, often with violence and in many cases abuse of drugs or alcohol. Job loss followed and dependence on benefits. Many were homeless for periods or living in hostels or poor accommodation. The incidence of violence and attendance in court was high and the incidence of Court appearances was very striking. Many who went to prison, on reflection perhaps should have been referred for treatment. There needs to be a programme in place for those being discharged from prison; many are in despair on release.

There was a high incidence of PTSD among "medics", many I knew and some were those from my unit in Germany. Those originating from Northern Ireland service provided the greatest number, possibly due to the repeated tours and the strain of the "unseen enemy". The Falklands campaign contributed a major group as did a little remembered campaign in Aden due to "Crater". The Gulf War produced a significant number of cases with those involved in the fighting the most severe. The PTSD symptoms of those affected by "Gulf War Syndrome" appear much less severe in its effect. However, the associated physical symptoms are very debilitating.

Discharge from the services places the onus for providing any treatment on the NHS which is not funded nor equipped to provide this care. There are no facilities in the UK to treat those in an acute state. They seek a sanctuary, they are afraid and desperate. The breakdown when it occurs is complete and dramatic. They have been to many clinics and have seen repeated consultants without continuity. They cannot relate to civilian therapists, with a belief that, as they have not experienced the horrors of war they cannot understand. There is no trust and no support and follow up. Many GP's are not aware of the condition and treat symptoms with drug therapy.

The War Pension is an issue of considerable angst to many. The awarding for PTSD has been very slow and varied. Many medical examinations, delays and endless forms result in a basic award, which then is challenged many times to attempt to have this increased. It is an endless battle to achieve what is a very basic sum. In 2007, the maximum possible war pension is £7,264.40 and the common starting point for a claim is only 20% of the full amount. There are well documented attempts to reduce the award claiming recovery or improvement. The conflict over the assessments awarded by the Benefits Agency and the War Pension Agency leave many bewildered. Recognition is what the majority seek not financial reward. Attendance at a tribunal is recommended for those who wish to see the system in action and the despair and frustration of those who are forced to rely on it.

Anger Management, Cognitive Behaviour Therapy and Counselling were the backbone of treatment for those with severe PTSD. Therapy is delayed by having to detoxify or stabilise the recipient and this can often take a week. There is little point in starting anything other than supportive therapy if drugs and alcohol are being abused. Gaining the confidence and trust of the casualty plays a large part in the preliminary proceedings. This regime helped many, but the pace of progress and the results were so variable that I doubted the efficacy. Measuring improvement demanded repeated testing and was in many cases subjective. The patient did not appear to recognise the improvement claimed through the scoring system assessment.

Following the closure of the hospital it very quickly became obvious that many had relied on it for support, which was not available through their local services. The removal of this resource had a considerable effect on their stability and many telephoned to ask, as did their relatives in many cases, how to get support. There remains a major requirement for a help line system, manned by those known and trusted, to reassure and support. My aim was to try and establish a voluntary system but this proved impossible. But I then was introduced to David Walters, and we met and discussed his ideas and proposals. I was sceptical and could find no reason to justify his training against any other method. However I was sufficiently interested to see what it could achieve and arranged some volunteers from those I knew needed help. This has now increased to the development of the protocol and six further sessions are planned. All who have taken part have benefited in some cases markedly. This assessment is judged on their own subjective reactions during and after the training. I have attended all sessions and have been impressed with the rapport development and interrelationship, the speed of getting to "core" issues and the progressive improvement as issues are addressed. There is a built-in method of sidelining issues which the patient does not wish to address. The "method" as it has now developed is non-invasive and non-confrontational. The relaxation techniques are very effective and many report dramatic improvements in sleep and freedom from nightmares. To see a troubled ex-serviceman cry with joy and relief as his "demons" have not appeared when he closed his eyes is a moving experience. "They are gone they do not exist". They remain gone and this PTSD casualty is now looking to a future with his family, re-united.

It is easy to become too enthusiastic when one wishes to see a technique which can assist sufferers come to terms and cope with PTSD. If it is possible then the benefits are enormous for a group which needs a new approach to treatment. The financial benefits and savings to society do not need to be elaborated upon. The benefit to the life of the ex-serviceman and his family cannot be overstated. It is early days and the pilot study is continuing with volunteers. Information is spread by texts and personal contact and through testimonials from those who have benefited and continue to use the techniques learned on the training programme.

As always funding is needed to train others in the techniques, to fund the clinics and a backup of support of trained personnel to provide the continuing link and reinforcement of the techniques. This is the next stage. Linking with a welfare agency to give assistance with housing and job applications and employment would complete a package which would return many to useful citizenship.

The Service and official welfare agencies are becoming overwhelmed by the requirement and may become swamped. It is perhaps time to look at a new methodology and review its ability to help those casualties of War.

In the next chapter we will see the affect of Post Traumatic Stress Disorder on individuals.

Dr W R Short CB CSt J MBChB FRCP(Glas) retired from the Royal Army Medical Corps in the rank of Major General having served as the Surgeon General British Army and former Director General, British Army Medical Services. Dr Short was a witness in the 2002 joint action case for the 1900 service personnel who claimed the MoD provided inadequate support for their PTSD. He now volunteers his time to support the ex-service personnel who are PTSD casualties and have received no effective support from any other agency in the UK.

CHAPTER 2

OVERVIEW OF PTSD

By
David Walters

Post Traumatic Stress Disorder (PTSD) has been described as "the mind's natural reaction to an abnormal experience". And anytime we experience traumatic situations, whether a threat to our own life or witnessing the death or mutilation of others, our conscious and subconscious mind experiences emotional shock. In just the same way as surgeons practice on cadavers to help them overcome the natural revulsion at cutting into human bodies, with training, we can overcome the conscious trauma – that's how military personnel, paramedics, fire fighters and police officers can do the jobs they do.

But most of this training is conducted at a conscious level. In the military part of the training is to dehumanise the enemy – that's why soldiers today still learn bayonet drill. When you get into close hand to hand combat the clinically sterile warfare of guided missiles and smart bombs gives way to the most primal of our instincts – kill or be killed. And I am pleased to report that this does not appear to be a natural state for the British veterans I have worked with. In fact a common trauma which needs to be released is the sense of guilt which the PTSD casualty feels about the dead person. In some cases the guilt is for their mates who were killed when they survived, in others the people in the "enemy" forces who had been killed or even innocent bystanders who the veteran feels they should have saved. All of these experiences place an emotional guilt into the subconscious of the individual.

The impact of the exposure to these traumatic events on the mind can be exceedingly damaging. Some people have either strong natural coping mechanisms or have developed their own personal techniques for releasing these memories. No one can tell who will be affected and who will escape. A column of soldiers walking down a street may be hit with small arms fire, a roadside bomb or a mortar attack – it is just luck who gets hit and who survives. No one criticises the casualties injured by bullets or shrapnel. It's accepted as a fact of war and they are given appropriate treatment for their injury.

In just the same way, the injury to the mind from witnessing and experiencing traumatic events causes casualties. In this case the injury is invisible. It is solely in the mind, but it is nonetheless a combat related injury, just the same as a bullet wound. The difference is that up till now we have stigmatised these casualties with terms such as shell shock, combat fatigue and now combat stress. In the past we shot these casualties for cowardice. Now we are more aware of the problem and actually provide some support. Although even today this is often in the form of a psychiatric discharge from the military. So if we can accept from this point forward that PTSD is an invisible injury to the mind, then these casualties deserve the same level of care and treatment as any other veteran physically injured in the service of their country.

It should be pointed out that PTSD is an extremely complex subject with many causes and various manifestations. In the very broadest terms we talk about three types of PTSD – acute, chronic and complex.

Firstly, to be diagnosed with PTSD the following symptoms must be present in the person –

a. The person has experienced or witnessed a life-threatening event and felt intense fear or horror.

b. The traumatic event is persistently re-experienced as memories, dreams or flashbacks

c. The person adopts avoidance strategies and numbing of responsiveness.

d. Increased arousal often in the form of sleep disturbance, outbursts of anger or hyper-vigilance.

e. The symptoms must last more than one month

f. The disturbance must cause significant impairment in social, work or other situations.

Also the duration of the symptoms is taken into account. Acute PTSD is where the symptoms last less than 3 months and chronic is where the symptoms last more than 3 months. Also PTSD can be considered "Delayed Onset" if the symptoms do not emerge in the first 6 months after the trauma. The final category of PTSD is known as "complex" PTSD. The clinical definition is that "co-morbidity or an Axis II disorder" exists along with the PTSD. In plain English that means that the PTSD casualty must have other problems such as alcoholism, drug abuse or suicidal tendencies, to name a few.

Acute PTSD could come from a civilian experiencing a life or death situation. This could be a traffic accident, a natural disaster, violent crime or rape. This traumatic event gets stored in the person's subconscious. Sometimes their natural coping mechanisms are not effective and the troubling memory from this event will start to intrude into their normal life. In the majority of people their natural coping mechanisms do work correctly and the traumatic memory will be collapsed. This normally happens, quite naturally, in the first 28 days after experiencing the traumatic event – the experiences in this period are sometimes called post traumatic stress response. However, if the nightmares, sleep disturbance, sense of loss or sadness and hyper-vigilance do not dissipate after 28 days, then the problem is more likely to be considered a disorder. In many cases acute PTSD can be released very quickly.

In some situations a recent event triggers a deep-seated trauma which may have been experienced during childhood. And these childhood traumas typically result from long-term physical, mental or sexual abuse. Often the abuse was conducted over a period of months and years, which embeds the trauma much deeper into the emotional core of the person. This form of PTSD will often last for long periods of time. If the symptoms persist for more than three months it is known as chronic PTSD.

This form of PTSD is often harder to release than the acute form because there are so many facets to the traumatic memory which are synthesised into a single representation of the event. This normally takes longer to resolve for two main reasons. Firstly there is a need to actually identify the core issue. The casualty may talk about the recent trauma and actually avoid or misdirect the intervention because of the deep-seated pain surrounding the core issue. And secondly, there will be many associations with the core memory each of which need to be isolated and subsequently collapsed.

Delayed onset PTSD can be particularly troubling because it doesn't manifest until long after the traumatic incident (a minimum of 6 months to be diagnosed as "delayed onset"). But this can often happen years after the event. A second life-threatening event, such as a car accident, can be all that is needed to trigger full-blown PTSD in a veteran many years after the original trauma. One word of caution needs to be said at this point. Many service personnel have already undergone personality and emotional changes by the time they return from a combat mission. This will be evident to family and friends but the PTSD casualty will either be confused about what is happening to them, or in denial about their problems. This is not delayed onset PTSD. It is most likely chronic

PTSD which has not yet been diagnosed.

The final form is complex PTSD. This form of PTSD is often a result of repeated exposure to traumatic incidents. This is typically found in military personnel who have repeated combat experience and emergency services personnel who have regularly responded to catastrophic events. Classic cases here would be the first responders attending the 7 July bus and tube bombings. They may have had many exposures to traumatic events in the past, but the scale and horror of this event overwhelmed their coping strategies and all the other suppressed events have surfaced to compound the problem. Although many people develop coping strategies for rationalising the conscious reaction to the trauma the deeper emotional reaction can be far harder to release.

The effects of complex PTSD are so profound that individuals who develop this form have extreme difficulty functioning in a normal way in society. It is common to find a string of failed relationships, alcohol and substance abuse, inability to maintain a job, homelessness and ultimately suicide amongst this casualty group. Almost 30,000 British personnel earned the South Atlantic Medal for service during the Falklands War. Of these 255 died in combat. In 2002, a BBC report suggested that a greater number than those who gave their lives in the Falklands have since committed suicide. This report argued that the high number of suicides among Falklands veterans arose because of the failure to effectively treat PTSD.

Signs and Symptoms of PTSD

The primary issue associated with PTSD is the frequency and intensity of the intrusive memories of the traumatic event. This can occur in the form of flashbacks and nightmares. These are frequently so intense that the casualty loses touch with reality and fully experiences the event as if they were actually reliving it. This has several consequences for the casualty. Firstly, behaviour appropriate to a combat zone is considered highly irregular in civilian society. At best this can lead to extreme embarrassment for the casualty, at worst the brutal murder of innocent bystanders. There are numerous reported incidents of soldiers being incarcerated for murder, only to be subsequently diagnosed with PTSD. Many PTSD casualties live in constant fear of experiencing a flashback when around their family members and causing them extreme physical harm.

The intensity of these intrusive recollections has been linked to the difficulty experienced by PTSD casualties in releasing the memory. One theory suggests that the memories are so intense when the casualty goes to sleep their normal sleeping patterns are disrupted by the nightmares. This stops the individual entering REM sleep, which is the time when our brain processes thoughts from short to long term memory. This interruption of the sleep process is what causes the intense images and feelings to remain in short term memory. If this is actually the case then helping these casualties experience a normal sleep cycle would help reduce the intensity of the PTSD symptoms.

Unfortunately many PTSD casualties are so disturbed when they sleep that they resort to self-medicating with alcohol or other substances to try and suppress the intrusive memories. This may appear to work in the short term, but a person passed out due to excessive alcohol does not experience a healthy, recuperative sleep pattern. They may be able to suppress the immediate nightmares but they obtain no therapeutic benefit from the sleep they do get. One PTSD casualty told me that he had been unable to close his eyes for over 25 years with out his "monsters" immediately appearing. Another stated that he knew of a Falklands veteran, a paratrooper, who had not slept between sunset and sunrise since leaving the islands. Obviously sleep disturbance of this level will have long-term psychological and physiological effects on the individual.

Research carried out in Israel on sleep deprivation found that even after just a short period of being denied REM sleep, the subjects quickly developed serious psychoses. Can you imagine the problems this causes for the PTSD casualty? Not only are they suffering from severe intrusive memories and nightmares, they are also being made more prone to developing secondary psychosis. These hallucinations, delusions and irrational thoughts further separate them from reality.

There are many PTSD casualties who have developed coping strategies that allow them to sleep through the night without the use of drugs or alcohol. But these coping mechanisms do nothing to relieve the other symptoms of PTSD, such as hyper-arousal. So this would tend to argue against the REM sleep disturbance as being a primary cause of PTSD.

Hyper-arousal is a common symptom of complex PTSD. This has nothing to do with sexual prowess. Rather the casualty experiencing these symptoms will often wildly overreact to a startling situation. A slamming door, dropped cutlery and even a car engine backfiring are enough to cause the casualty to dive for cover. Some report that they can never walk in front of an exposed window in their homes and others develop defensive behaviours such as going "on patrol" late at night and early morning to check the perimeter (of their homes) are clear.

In extreme cases, casualties can find themselves falling into escape and evasion mode, running out of situations they perceive to be hostile and going to ground for days or even weeks on end. In one case, the casualty's anxiety was triggered at a party. He returned home, packed his kit in the back of his car and went to ground. It took nearly four months for him to regain the sense of stability and security to return to his family home.

In an attempt to compensate for the nightmares, psychosis and hyper-arousal, PTSD casualties often experience emotional shutdown. This is a natural self-defence mechanism. The experience is just so raw and intense that they are unable to re-experience the situation and maintain any degree of socially acceptable function. Casualties in this mode will be extremely unresponsive to normal everyday situations, they will communicate monosyllabically with their spouses and family and they will withdraw from any form of social interaction. The casualty may not even be aware that they have entered this mode. But the spouse will see this as a form of rejection. Initially they will try and engage their loved one, who will often feel more threatened by this attempt at intimacy and withdraw even further.

Over time, this emotional shutdown will start to cause a sense of resentment in the spouse which in turn will lead to a lower tolerance for the abnormal behaviour being exhibited by the casualty. When you then add into the mix the disturbed sleep patterns, the possible excessive use of alcohol, violent mood swings, flashbacks, nightmares and hyper-arousal, the relationship is put under incredible strain. In a large number of cases this strain is just too much and the relationship quickly fails. It is not uncommon for a casualty with complex PTSD to experience numerous failed relationships including several failed marriages.

Ultimately the PTSD casualty sees their world fail around them and unless given effective support and treatment, many PTSD casualties succumb to their untreated mind injury and die at their own hand.

The Extent of PTSD

Research by the National Centre for Post Traumatic Stress Disorder in the US indicates that there is a 7.8% chance that a member of the adult population will suffer from PTSD. This breaks down to 10.4% for women and 5.0% for men. When you compare this to the lifetime probability of experiencing a traumatic incident of 60.7% for men and 51.2% for women you can see than a man experiencing a single traumatic event will have a 1 in 12 chance of developing PTSD. A woman has a 1 in 5 chance.

The research then goes on to report that among Vietnam combat veterans there was 30.9% chance among male veterans and 26.9% chance among female veterans. An additional 22.5% of male veterans and 21.2% of female veterans developed partial PTSD. So the overall prevalence of PTSD for Vietnam veterans was 53.4% for men and 48.1% for women. 12 years after the Vietnam War ended (an average of 15 years after exposure for the service person) 15.2% of male and 8.1% of female veterans were still diagnosed with PTSD.

Bringing these figures closer to home, a report in 1991 indicated that 22% of Falklands veterans were suffering from PTSD although other figures report this to be as low as 9%. During the Falklands campaign, 255 British servicemen died in action and according to a BBC report in 2002, more than this number (possibly as many as 350) have died by their own hand. But taking the lower 9% figure, up to 2,700 Falklands veterans could be at risk from PTSD.

How are they helped now?

The support to British PTSD casualties is patchy to say the least. Many hundreds, if not thousands, are casualties and don't even know it. These can often stem back to the Second World War and Korea. They accept that what is happening to them is a normal part of the ex-serviceman's life and they just get on with it. They're from a generation when men were expected to be the strong silent types. So they don't talk about their problems. They just suffer in silence, coping as best they can, often with alcohol as a constant companion.

Another group are in denial. Their behaviour has changed, their relationships have failed and serial divorce is the norm for these people. Although those around them can point to the problems, the casualties themselves cannot acknowledge what is going on. So they also don't seek help. As their condition worsens and their ability to cope reduces they become less and less able to maintain themselves in normal society. These people often end up homeless, sleeping rough or in prison. There as some astounding statistics relating to this group.

Approximately 7% of the UK prison population is ex-military, that's around 5,600 inmates. Not all of these are PTSD casualties, some are just criminals who happened to have served in the military.

Now let's look at another subculture - the homeless. Many PTSD casualties find it so difficult to remain functional in normal society that they end up homeless or sleeping rough. Statistics vary but it is estimated that 0.4% of our population are homeless (living in hostels, bed and breakfast, squats and on friends' floors). This is over 230,000 people. Recent government figures indicate that less than 500 people are sleeping rough in our community, but some charities suggest the figure could be closer to 1200. Now what is most alarming is that some estimates show that between 25 and 30% of these people are ex-military. This means that over 58,000 ex-servicemen are homeless and between 125 and 300 are living on the streets. How many of theses are PTSD casualties? How many of the people sleeping rough in our towns and cities are suffering from violent flashbacks and nightmares about their combat experience?

Others may seek medical attention for their symptoms, but they can commonly be misdiagnosed and treated for depression and anxiety. Although the medication may reduce the intensity of the symptoms, it does nothing to resolve the underlying issues. And so these casualties spend their life heavily medicated, constant users of scarce NHS resources with no hope of long-term recovery.

Some lucky ones are correctly diagnosed with PTSD. And some do receive effective treatment for their condition. Others receive counselling and respite care through a variety of service charities. But there is little evidence to suggest that this actually provides long-term relief from the symptoms of PTSD. Those who do recover often have acute or chronic PTSD, while those with complex PTSD receive very little in the way of effective treatment. In fact the NHS acknowledges that they have neither the capacity nor capability for dealing with complex PTSD in military veterans.

So where does this leave our veterans? And what can be done to help these people get their lives back and become productive members of society once again?

Before we look at a possible solution we need to get a better understanding of the real situation for the first hand experience of those working with these casualties. In chapter 3, Martin Kinsella, the Chief Executive of P3, the social inclusion charity, will tell us about his experience dealing with homeless ex-servicemen.

David Walters is a former Royal Navy submarine Officer who now leads a growing company specialising in the area of workplace stress resilience. During his extensive experience working in the nuclear power industry in North America as an emergency management consultant and in multinational corporations as a crisis management consultant he developed a keen interest in the effect of operational stress on first responders. This led him to research many methods for overcoming stress. From this he developed a technique known as "The Walters Method™" for teaching people to become resilient to stress. A variant of this method has been used to good effect in teaching veterans how to overcome their symptoms of PTSD.

CHAPTER 3

HOMELESSNESS: THE EX-SERVICES DIMENSION

By
Martin Kinsella

Official figures show that around 24,000 people leave the armed forces each year. Within this number there are a group of individuals who have served in the armed forces for a significant period and find the transition to civilian life very challenging, these people are at risk of becoming homeless. There is another group of service leavers at similar risk, these are personnel who have either failed basic training or have been administratively or medically discharged. Up to 98% of ex-services homeless people are thought to be ex-army and the same percentage are thought to be male. This of course doesn't mean that the needs of the RAF, Navy and female ex-service homeless can be ignored, indeed it demands that special care should be taken in meeting their specific needs.

Research (i) by the New Policy Institute and Crisis, the homelessness charity, has estimated that there are between 310,000 and 380,000 single homeless people in the UK at any one time with less than 1,000 of these being rough sleepers. Around a quarter of the 310,000 to 380,000 are housed temporarily in hostels, B&Bs or are in imminent threat of eviction from precariously held tenancies by reason of rent debt and/or general inability to manage and maintain relationships or an independent tenancy. It has been further estimated (ii) that the broad annual cost in terms of unemployment amongst this group in terms of lost income, lost tax to the state and welfare benefit payments was £600 million in 2004, this equates to around £660 million in 2007, given a notional annual 3% rise. It is widely thought that many single homeless people would wish to work, given the right support and opportunities.

How many homeless people have a military background? The answer is that we cannot say categorically, what we do know however is, that given the figures for single homeless above, we can say with certainty there are today significant numbers of homeless ex-military personnel. Some research studies have suggested that up to 30% of single homeless people are ex-military: *'we are still looking at a homeless ex-service population of up to 100,000'* (iii) whilst others suggest that the figure is more like 5% (iii). Even if the latter of these figures 5% is taken to be correct and the figure above of between 310,000 and 380,000 single homeless is rounded down to 300,000 then we still have a conservative estimate of 15,000 homeless ex-service personnel in our midst. I would like to suggest that as always the true figure is somewhere in the middle, moreover even if it were 15,000 then this is 15,000 too many.

Where are they tonight?

One organisation that specifically targets homeless ex-service personnel is Ex-Service Fellowship Centres (EFC). EFC provides a direct access 57 bed hostel that aims to, where possible, provide an immediate accommodation based option to rough sleeping; the hostel is in London. EFC state on their website (v) that in the year 2005-2006 they: *'provided 19,379 nights of accommodation for veterans who would otherwise have been on the streets!'* This equates to 54 veterans each night of the year. EFC should be congratulated on this important work.

The EFC website goes on to say:

The main problem we encounter is HOMELESSNESS and in this regard we are the only Service charity, south of the border, that offers ex-Service homeless IMMEDIATE refuge from the streets if it is within our ability to do so.

Other non ex-service homelessness service provider organisations up and down the country including P3 provide services on a daily basis to service veterans. However I am sure that the number of veterans receiving a service is nowhere near the number that needs one. Another study (vi) found that 51% of ex-service people had given up looking for accommodation, 63% had slept rough in the previous 12 months and that 41% chose not to stay in hostels. It should be remembered that military training includes being trained to sleep rough and that 21% of veterans questioned stated that they did not need help whilst 40% admitted to an alcohol problem. This research dates from 1997 and some will say things have improved in the last ten years, that may be the case, however any improvement in the co-ordination of support services for the ex–military needs to be weighed against the ongoing need of the 24,000 additional service leavers each year.

Defining the need

Case Study 1

R, an ex-soldier, has been engaged with a wide range of services for approximately six years. He originally became homeless following a relationship breakdown; his wife was unable to deal with his gambling problem, additionally he had an alcohol dependency and some assessed mental health issues including anxiety and paranoia. R was admitted to a direct access hostel.

External support for R's range of needs was sought and he periodically engaged. An all too typical Catch-22 situation existed, that is until R addressed his alcohol and behaviour problems the external specialist project that could assist him in tackling his gambling problem refused to accept him.

Eventually funding was approved and he successfully completed an alcohol detoxification programme and transferred to planned move-on accommodation whilst waiting for a place on a gambling programme. However, once he moved in he could not cope with his situation and without warning abandoned his new accommodation and left the area.

Case Study 2

P, who served in Bosnia, has been in prison for offences committed to support his use of a number of drugs. At the start of his contact with P3 he was difficult to communicate with and would not trust or engage with his support staff. However due to the persistence of his support team he successfully completed a drug programme and eventually began to build relationships. He has now successfully moved to his own accommodation and has resumed contact with his family after a gap of some years.

Case Study 3

G had been dishonourably discharged from the army. His behaviour, presentation and communication led support staff to seek a formal mental health assessment. G was diagnosed with schizophrenia, representations to the military authorities were made and G had his dishonourable discharge revoked, full backdated reinstatement of his military pension rights and other wage payments were made and he was able to access Disability Living Allowance for the first time. At first the change of circumstances was overwhelming for G, however after a time with the right support G was able to establish a more settled and better quality way of life in his own accommodation.

The following case studies are taken from the Ex-Service Fellowship Centres' Annual Report 2006.

Case Study 4 (vii)

T, an ex-Army sergeant, was so filthy after living on the streets for 11 years that it took a day for him to get clean. He was a chaotic street drinker with a history of mental health problems. As is usual, the charity provided T with new clothing. Once cleaned up, T put his new clothes on. Sadly, the next morning he appeared in his old clothes, despite the fact they had been thrown in a bin … he had sold the new clothes for drink. Needless to say, the staff started over again. Initially, T couldn't sleep on the bed but slept on the floor and as a hardened street drinker he found life in NBH, which is a dry hostel, doubly difficult. After many months of care and support, T began to function much better than anyone thought possible and was able to cope with daily life in a "normal" situation. The good news is that he has moved on to a supported housing scheme and is still there.

Case Study 5 (vii)

S is an ex-infantry man who served in a Scottish regiment. Over the years, EFC had provided a roof over his head, money, a listening ear and clothing. However, his problems related to his severe drug habit and his violent temper that he could barely control. His chaotic and aggressive behaviour had all but barred him from most sources of help but he knew that if things were really bad, he could find some support from the EFC offices in Victoria. He was sleeping rough in a sleeping-bag one night when he was attacked by a group of well-dressed young men. He fought back but was subsequently arrested and charged after the group claimed he had attacked them. S protested his innocence but the police were not interested because he had a criminal record for violence. S became desperate, as he could not face another spell in prison. One afternoon he came in and stated bluntly that he could take the pressure no longer and he was going to kill himself. He was crying like a baby. The EFC team, with SSAFA Homeless Division support, swung into action ... suffice it to say S is still alive and in supported accommodation. The charges were later dropped as the complainants did not turn up for the court case!

Case Study 6 (vii)

D had served two years with the colours. He settled well in civilian life and had a good job in local government. After eight years his partner died and in his grief, D landed up on the streets. His family background involved drug use and sadly, he sought respite in heroin and crack cocaine. He arrived at EFC's Victoria office one horrid February morning, so cold that he could hardly speak. When he recovered he was admitted to NBH on the clear understanding that it was a drug-free facility. He wanted to recover so he was willing to try and live in the hostel without drugs. Over a period of four months, the staff worked very hard to get D off heroin but it was too strong for him despite even the involvement of specialist drug workers. D returned to the streets to feed his habit...the NBH staff were devastated when they heard that he died from an "overdose" a week later...he was only 32. Some time after the event the NBH staff received a letter from D's mother thanking the staff for trying to help. In parting she said that D had been really grateful for the kindness and compassion he had been shown while at NBH. In the end, the problem had been just too enormous for him.

Case Study 7 (vii)

Want your brass work cleaned? E had been on the streets for a number of years as a result of a very unhappy marriage. Despite his street time, he had recovered enough to start getting his life back on track and he came to EFC to try and find a way to do so. After a discussion, he struck on the idea of starting a brass cleaning business in central London...he said his Army career had provided him with the specialist trade knowledge! E asked for, and was given, a letter of introduction from EFC to potential customers. It explained that he was a veteran trying to get his life back together. This was important as his dreadlocks were not what people expected to see on a soldier. We are pleased to say, that the Victoria office still has calls from potential customers willing to give E work if we can vouch for him. He is doing well and has, by any standard, reclaimed his life.

We cannot categorically state that all these cases were due to the impact of PTSD. But the experiences of these veterans which brought them to homelessness – alcohol abuse, drug usage, matrimonial breakdown, violent outbursts and inability to relate to civilian society are all common symptoms experienced by PTSD casualties. The question I ask the reader is how many of these cases could and should have been avoided by the right services being available at the right time? I believe that a timely early intervention would have resulted in a better prognosis in each of these cases and that the time where we can tolerate the right services at the right time not being made available has come and gone. I ask you to lend your weight and influence to our cause by making it known to your political representatives that you expect the best available services to be made accessible and available to our ex-military personnel in a timely fashion in their hour of need.

In the next chapter we will look in more detail at the case of a young Royal Marine whose life collapsed into a nightmare of drug and alcohol abuse after his return from the Falklands war.

Martin Kinsella MA is Chief Executive of P3 the social inclusion charity. P3 was judged to be the 2005 UK Charity of the Year in the Charity Times UK Charity Awards. P3 was recently awarded the number 1 spot in the 2007 Sunday Times Top 100 Best Companies to work for list. More information on the charity can be found at www.p3charity.com.

(i) Kenway P. and Palmer G. (2003) *HOW MANY, HOW MUCH?*: single homelessness and the question of numbers and cost, Crisis.
(ii) Crisis (2004) *Hidden Homelessness: Britain's Invisible City*. Crisis.
(iii) Balintyne S. and Hanks S. (2000) *Lest We Forget: ex-servicemen and homelessness*, Crisis
(iv) Dandeker C. et al (2005) *Feasibility Study On The Extent, Causes, Impact and Costs Of Rough Sleeping and Homelessness Amongst Ex- Service Personnel in a Sample of Local Authorities in England*, King's Centre for Military Health Research, King's College London.
(v) www.exsfc.org.uk
(vi) Gunner G and Knott H. (1997) *Homeless on Civvy Street, Ex-Service Action Group*
(vii) www.exsfc.org.uk

CHAPTER 4

NUMBING THE PAIN

By
David Walters

POST TRAUMATIC STRESS DISORDER

We are the secret casualties
The walking, talking wounded

No visible scars
Missing limbs
Or sightless eyes
Just sudden starts
Wakeful nights
Mood shifts
And numbed emotions

We cope with life
As if it's just spilt milk
Mopped up, wrung out
Then swilled away

We carefully unwrap old memories

As if they are too fragile
Or too awful to examine

Victimised by our own dreams
We forever re-live old horrors

Cherishing life
Yet unafraid of death

Somehow dead
While still alive

Mick Furey

In the last chapter we read about the problems that veterans of the British Armed Forces are suffering and how this can lead to homelessness. We saw how between 15,000 and possibly as many as 100,000 ex-service personnel need to use shelters and temporary accommodation and how charitable organisations such as P3, the social inclusion charity, Crisis and the Ex-Services Fellowship Centres are working to meet these needs. In the next few chapters we will discover in more detail how veterans returning from the Falklands have suffered. How their lives have changed because of PTSD and more importantly the impact that this is having on their minds, their families, their friends and ultimately our society as a whole. In the following case studies we have changed the names of those concerned to protect their privacy.

Bill joined the Royal Navy as a junior stoker. Coming from a troubled family he saw the navy as a means of escaping the abusive relationship he had with his father. But joining his first ship, he quickly found himself in trouble for the aggressive way he responded to the teasing of the other ratings in his mess deck. It was not long before he found himself in detention quarters for insubordination. On his return from detention he requested to transfer to the Royal Marines. This was denied. Bill was an athletic individual and a good runner who had represented his ship in various sporting events. So it was not long before his temper and immaturity again earned him a visit to detention quarters. This time his request for the Royal Marines was accepted and he transferred in the mid 1960's.

During the 1970's Bill completed several tours of duty in Northern Ireland including some extended periods in observation posts whilst working in support of Special Forces. A typical Marine, he worked hard and played hard. He was a very fit man and he prided himself in his physical ability and his endurance in difficult times. As is often the case with Marines, he received a number of injuries including broken ribs, wrist and ankle from training accidents. In common with many servicemen he smoked heavily and drank in moderation during the week. But at weekends, when not required for duty or operations, he would do what most sailors and Marines did - that is have a "good run ashore".

In 1982 during the Falklands War, Bill was deployed along with the rest of his Marine Company to the Falklands. He first experienced the real fear of the Falklands as they were being bombed on the way into landing on the islands.

Like many soldiers and Marines unaccustomed to being confined between decks on a ship, he found the need to remain in an enclosed space while being attacked to be a strain that he could not bear. During at least one attack he found himself in panic trying to escape from the lower decks of the ship to get on to the upper deck where he felt some sense of safety. His strong streak of insubordination again showed itself and he would often make his way to the upper deck during air attacks to avoid his fear of being between decks.

Bill stepped ashore at Port San Carlos and with the rest of his company started to dig in and commence patrolling in preparation for the push to Port Stanley. Although under no illusions about the fight which lay ahead, the initial time on the island was relatively quiet. They had been under the impression that the Argentinean conscripts were suffering from low morale, skill and leadership. But it was during the attack on Mount Harriet, when one marine was killed and over 20 wounded that Bill started to experience real fear. He continued to do his duty, proud of being a Marine but feeling an increasing sense of dread with each step closer to Port Stanley. And an increasing sense of shame about his growing fear, and guilt that he was uninjured when friends and comrades had been killed and wounded. On the night of the ceasefire he got extremely drunk.

Then the nightmares started.

Returning home from the Falklands War he tried to keep control of by throwing himself into action and volunteered for a deployment to Northern Ireland. But his performance was seen as erratic and when he returned from his deployment he was taken off front line duties. As time progressed his health deteriorated. Bill suffered a succession of minor illnesses and ailments, which one medical officer suggested could have been due to suppressed emotions from his Falklands experience. Eventually he felt that he could no longer perform as a Marine, his confidence and health had deteriorated and so he applied for his discharge.

With the money he had from his discharge and his pension he bought in to a pub with a woman he had known for some years. At first things seemed to be going well. But during the late 1980s his flashbacks and symptoms of PTSD worsened. It was then he started to drink heavily and consistently. From leaving the Marines until the mid 1990's, Bill had been drinking heavily until he was suffering from full-blown alcoholism as he attempted to use alcohol to self-medicate to reduce the painful memories and nightmares associated with his PTSD. He ended up drinking much of the profits from his pub, the relationship with his partner failed and eventually she kicked him out. Now homeless and drifting, he found the effectiveness of alcohol reduced; he then turned to drugs. He used a wide variety of drugs ranging from cannabis to speed, ecstasy, cocaine, anti-depressants and sleeping pills. Bill sought help for his alcoholism and joined Alcoholics Anonymous. Eventually he managed to dry out but without the use of alcohol to self medicate against his nightmares and flashbacks, his drug consumption continued to increase. During this period of his life Bill's emotions became increasingly unstable.

He said he found it difficult to identify with the real world and his real emotions. He continued to rely on both illicit and prescription drugs to hold himself together. Bill was living in a hostel and actually making some money from doing odd jobs and part time work. Once he had successfully dried out he started to put his life back in order and he was referred to psychotherapy due to an increasing number of issues which he had been unable to deal with. Although he did not continue this treatment because he felt that the civilian medical team didn't understand what he was going through. They didn't know what it was like to be in military combat. They didn't know how to communicate with a Marine. He received little effective support from the NHS and actually paid for hypnotherapy to help him with his psychological condition. Although this provided some relief, he had to stop because he could not afford the treatment.

He was now experiencing more flashbacks and regularly "went on patrol" making serious preparations to kill those people he felt were a threat to him. His chaotic condition brought about by his PTSD was made even worse by the effects of the cocktail of drugs he was taking to suppress his nightmares and flashbacks. He began to engage in violent and criminal activity to feed his drug habit. This made him feel even worse about himself and the dishonour he had brought upon himself and the Royal Marines.

A large part of his feeling regarding his experiences during the Falklands was shame and guilt due to the fear that he felt when under attack. He now felt that he needed to be shamed. He began to get involved in physical, emotional and sexually self-destructive practices and was eventually arrested for indecent exposure. As a result of this he was seen by a social worker and psychiatrist. He subsequently missed his appointment at a specialist clinic for PTSD because he felt embarrassed about the reason for being arrested. In addition to his sense of shame he felt guilty about those who died in the war while he had come through physically unharmed. He also felt impotent to control his emotions. He tried to compensate in his life by exerting abusive power over those he came into contact with. This need for power and control resulted in paranoid episodes where he felt that people in the hostel were trying to kill him. His response, as is the case with many PTSD casualties, was to prepare for violent confrontation. Bill stated that he could kill and would do so if needed. His social worker agreed that he was becoming more dangerous. And although Bill wanted to enter a private facility specialising in veterans' post traumatic stress disorder his local NHS trust would not fund his attendance.

Bill moved away from the city. After spending time living in a tent he began to regain some control in his life and managed to take himself off drugs. He led an extremely controlled life taking obsessive precautions to avoid anything that could remind him of the Marines or the war. He continued in the self-imposed isolation until the anniversary of the Falklands War. Then he had a major relapse. He managed to obtain some emergency funding through a veterans charity which paid for a one week in patient assessment of his condition at a private hospital specialising in veterans PTSD. He received some support but without long-term funding he was again left to his own devices to regain control of his life. Bill has lived for the last several years on an emotional roller coaster. He has managed to avoid using alcohol or other drugs to self-medicate to numb the pain of his PTSD. But in making this decision he has subjected himself to violent anger and mood swings, terrifying nightmares and a constant risk of violence or injury to those around him. Like many PTSD veterans Bill has adopted the life of a semi-recluse unable to live in the world. But receiving no effective treatment from the medical community and living a life of shame and guilt because of the lack of control he feels over his own rage and anger.

Bill has managed through his own efforts to control his alcohol and drug abuse and he has also been able enter into a relationship with a woman who he feels has given him something to live for, although he also feels he does not deserve her. Bill's story could be that of any number of ex-servicemen. Feeling a sense of betrayal from their government and the unit they served because of the lack of support for their PTSD. While at the same time feeling disgust for the depths they stoop to through alcoholism and drug abuse as they attempt to self-medicate. Feelings of guilt regularly encompass them because they survived and feelings of shame and self-loathing for betraying the honour of their unit. Bill continues in this living hell, living the life of a near recluse on a knife edge between violent rage on one hand and suicidal despair on the other.

In the next chapter we will explore just how much damage PTSD does to the families and loved ones of the returning veteran.

CHAPTER 5

MORE INNOCENT VICTIMS

By
David Walters

DREAMS

Dreams still haunt me, invading my privacy,
Your worst imaginable nightmare without any piracy,
Invading your mind, unimaginable screams begin to corrupt,
Waking yourself your mind caught in a moment, your vision abstract.

Remembering events that you would rather just forget,
Suicide eventually becomes something you would not regret,
And then you must think of the others who are part of your "life",
Perhaps you have sons or daughters, if you are lucky you still have a wife.

Ever thought of the impact you have had on them? Your own kin,
Imagine your daughter screaming in the night and it being your sin,
Look around you at the mayhem you've caused due to your screaming in the night,
Then look at them and explain to your seven year old why she had such a fright.

Able bodied, yes, you are not that bad, now try walking in the street,
Those you meet wonder why you are not working, physically able, on your feet,
Yet the prospect of working fills your mind with such fear,
Looking back at your wrecked past with nothing to hold dear.

Maybe you will manage to get off state benefits, maybe you wont,
It becomes a bit of a joke when you keep trying despite being told "don't"
Over one hundred and forty jobs, more than many have in a lifetime,
What you have read is a portrayal of my "life" read in rhyme.

So despite trying and trying again, you're left to rot,
Anger at the betrayal after giving all to the melting pot,
The betrayal there, in your face each and every way,
Everyone who is anyone saying simply "just go away".

MW, RN

In the first case study we saw how easily it was for the veteran suffering from PTSD to slip into the habit of self-medicating with alcohol and other drugs to numb the pain of PTSD. In this chapter we look at how wide the impact of PTSD is, affecting not only the immediate casualty but also the family, friends and acquaintances of the veteran. Here is Dave's story in his own words.

I served as a Combat Medical Technician with 55 Field Surgical Team attached to 2 Field Hospital serving in the Falklands. I was at Port Stanley and moved to Fitzroy on Sir Galahad where we were bombed. I was on the tank deck awaiting disembarkation when the air strike happened and the bomb went of behind me and to my left. I was sitting on the front bumper of a Landrover which shielded me from most of the blast. I just received a flash burn on my left hand. At first I was confused and disoriented and angry that the ship had turned off its lights (as I thought at the time). Actually the bomb had exploded and filled the tank deck with smoke. As reality crept in I understood that we had been hit. It was then I realised that I had to act and do my job as a medic. As the smoke started to clear I could see people running round, confused, hurt, screaming and shouting. I gathered to me what medics were available and proceeded to work on the wounded.

It was obvious that the fire was spreading and in the centre of the tank deck was a pile of munitions waiting to be disembarked. Basically a giant bomb waiting to explode! The exits to the rear were out of action so we had to move forward with our casualties. Whilst finding access to the boat deck along the bulkhead there was a guy very badly injured. He was disembowelled; one leg was off above the knee, the other missing below the knee. He was waving his arms and asking for help. I knew there was nothing I could do for him so I had to make a decision and I left him. I just walked past him with my casualty. I've felt guilt and regret for 25 years that I didn't even say anything to him.

I came to the bottom of a stairwell and I saw two young Welsh guardsmen. They obviously didn't think they were going to make it out. They shook each others hands, pointed their rifles to each others head and pulled their triggers. There was nothing I could have done to stop them. It was their decision. When I thought back about this incident I just felt so disgusted with myself that I'd felt no sympathy, remorse or other emotion and they killed each other in front of my eyes.

Eventually we gained access to the boat decks and continued performing our job. We were Casevaced ashore and re-kitted. I was then sent back to Fitzroy to work with the surgical team where I performed triage duties. I spent the rest of the Falklands war working with that unit. After the war ended we flew to RAF Lynham. My wife met me and we were driven back to our unit. At first I was happy to be home. We started to pick up our relationship where we had left off before the Falklands. My wife was pleased that I was home and relieved that I had come through physically without serious injury. Neither of us knew that I was a casualty of PTSD.

It took a while for the changes to manifest themselves. The first was that I increased my alcohol intake and was on the slippery steps to self medication. It was a number of years before people started to tell me that I needed to be checked out because I was not the same person I used to be. I was becoming disruptive and my marriage suffered and ended in divorce. I was given a sideways posting as the army saw I was having problems and my career was effectively over. I left the army in 1989 to allow my wife to pursue her career. I was living with my wife in her hometown of Liverpool. I was doing the usual crappy jobs ex-servicemen end up with – security guard, carrying cash, petrol station attendant, storesman – nothing to do with my professional trade at all. It was such a waste.

My wife was being successful in her job but I was getting worse. I was self medicating with alcohol and recreational drugs such as cannabis. I was now being verbally abusive, arrogant, condescending and patronising. Basically I was pushing her away. The more she resented my behaviours the more I presented them. I just kept pushing her away. I didn't want people near me in case I lost them. I'd lost too many mates on the Sir Galahad – I didn't want to lose any more who were close to me. I know my wife still loved me and I loved her. I still didn't realise that I had this condition that was causing me to push her away. She decided that she'd had enough and moved out to get her own flat. She then filled for divorce for irreconcilable breakdown of the relationship and my pedantic behaviour. I didn't contest the divorce because it was what she wanted and even though there were still feelings between us.

I then moved back to Bradford to be close to my family because I needed support. My wife came to visit me about a year later. I think she still loved me, she just needed closure. It wasn't her fault she just couldn't cope with my problems.

Since then I have had 8 successive short term relationships which all ended in breakdown. I have had one long term relationship since the Falklands. It lasted nearly 10 years but we didn't live together, it was only part time. That's why I think it lasted so long. That relationship just dried up and fizzled out. I didn't know my behaviours were so destructive because they were sub-conscious. I wasn't even aware at what I was doing.

I became self employed so I could work when I wanted to. I learned how to forget anniversaries - mine, the war and my family. I then entered into another relationship which lasted 2 years. We went away travelling and got as far as Crete and then we found out that she was pregnant so we returned to the UK. It was an exact repeat of the emotional situation I had with my first wife. The closer she tried to get to me the worse I became towards her. After my daughter was born she didn't want her brought up in the destructive environment I was creating so she left. One day she left our home and went round to her friends where she called the police telling them that I was trying to kill our daughter. I had put my daughter in our car to take her to her grandparents – all of a sudden the car was surrounded by armed police – I was charged with threats to kill and false imprisonment because I'd locked the car door. That's all they could bring against me. This caused a build up of tension between me and my family. They had seen my behaviour deteriorating and so they believed her and wouldn't give me any support. So I told them I would have nothing to do with them. That was the last time I had any contact with my parents.

But that was when I had my first suicide attempt. I was drunk and planned to jump the central reservation on the Motorway but I crashed on the way there and realised that the van wouldn't make it that far. I just couldn't cope with the emotional and psychological pressure any more. I realised something was wrong and I went to seek professional help. That's when I was diagnosed with PTSD. After six months the charges against me were dropped. I was not allowed to see my daughter at all during that period. We then got stuck in the mire of family law. My partner wouldn't honour the court orders allowing me to see my daughter but the police wouldn't do anything. I was in town and I saw my partner. Because I hadn't seen my daughter for weeks I crossed over to see her and that night the police burst in to my home and arrested me for breaking my bail conditions – just because I wanted to say hello to my daughter. She's still breaking the court orders to let me have telephone contact with my daughter.

I then had to start dealing with the loss of my daughter, my parents and my partner, dealing with the judiciary and the system at large. I was getting no support from anyone from any welfare or medical organisation. And once I was diagnosed with PTSD it was like the lid was off – Pandora's Box was open - my symptoms got much worse. I also had developed agoraphobia and would only go out at night to stock up with alcohol. So I tried to kill myself again. This time with an overdose of the pills the psychiatric team had prescribed for me after my first attempt. They were just repeating the prescriptions and I was saving them up. I wouldn't be here if it wasn't for my nephew. He came round to see me on chance and couldn't get in so he called for an ambulance and a neighbour broke in a downstairs window and he found me. I was pretty out of it. I remember being woken up by the paramedics and I told them fuck off so they did. My nephew called my brother in law who came round. He took all the medication and alcohol and left me to sleep it off. I received no medical support at all after that attempt.

Since then I've had one final relationship which lasted 12 months but she was dysfunctional and we were just feeding each others problems. As result of this relationship I ended up penniless and homeless. I spent time living out of the YMCA and am now renting.

I went through a huge period of learning and the first psychiatrist I saw recommended that I contact Combat Stress. I was disgusted when I went there because I was given no treatment – just a week's respite care and then I was kicked out. Then I had to find something for my own wellbeing and it took a long time. It took nearly 4 years before the NHS recognised me as someone who needed help and referred me to a psychologist. After this I was assessed and referred to a psychiatric support team. I got some good work done.

The more I learned about PTSD, human psychology and myself as a PTSD casualty I was able to discern the destructive pattern that had become the core of my life. I had so much pent up rage I would re-direct my anger at anyone who came close to me. This led to highly inappropriate behaviour in the form of violent outbursts and verbal aggression. The targets for this aggression were those closest to me, the ones who were really trying to get close to me to help. But the closer they got, the more vulnerable I became and the greater my anger. I realised then my self defence radar was operating 360 degrees at full power 24/7. My self defence philosophy was based on the principle – before you can hurt me – I'm going to hurt you. I was operating in a state of constant alert – anticipating every word or action to be an attack directed towards me. I would never let people finish their sentences. I immediately assumed what they were saying was slight and so I would retaliate even before they had finished speaking.

The behaviour made people retreat from me so that I could not hurt them. But the further they retreated the more I felt slighted. I had lost so many friends and comrades in Sir Galahad I didn't want any more loss in my life. This made my sense of vulnerability even worse which increased the intensity of my subconscious self defence behaviour. So I was spiralling down in a self perpetuating cycle of aggression, withdrawal, perceived loss, increased feeling of vulnerability which in turn led to more aggression. I lost the ability to know what was true and what was just my paranoia. I felt that I was being attacked physically, psychologically and emotionally. I just didn't have any resources left to control my behaviour.

The more hurt I felt, the more I needed to be in a relationship to give me some degree of comfort. But as soon as the person got close to me I would feel vulnerable and the cycle would start all over again. This is how I entered and failed in 8 relationships in short succession. After each failure I just felt worse about myself, more rejected, heightening my sense of loss, making me feel more vulnerable and in need. It was during this destructive period of my life that I had my next two suicide attempts.

But because I was having problems with my daughter's mother and all the legal battle over custody I had to do a lot of work on myself. I qualified as a counsellor, parenting coach, anger management consultant, life coach, massage therapist and facilitator for the expert patient programme. I was slowly progressing with my own psychological intervention to deal with my own symptoms. I was taking sleeping tablets every night but often they wouldn't work and I'd have the nightmares. Until recently I've been living on my own as a relative recluse. It was safer for me and others that way. I now have a job and have recently made significant progress in learning how to effectively control the symptoms of my PTSD.

Dave's story gives us a good insight into the problems the families of veterans can face when their loved one returns home a casualty of PTSD. This destructive situation is extremely common with PTSD casualties and multiple failed relationships is the norm, not the exception. So how much is PTSD really costing our society? What is the real cost of all these failed marriages, broken homes and fatherless children?

Our next case study will look at the life of one Falklands veteran who was not able to control his violent behaviour resulting from his PTSD.

CHAPTER 6

A GROWING POPULATION

By
David Walters

PTSD ONE

What is this feeling?
That hangs on

Is it the fear of Battle?

Trapped in the maelstrom of dread and passion
Catching the heat

Nay . . . 'tis not

Is it the fear of Cowardliness?

That foulness of all panic
Stealing ones very ego
Leaving a barren shell

Nay . . . 'tis not

Is it the fear of Death?

Singling not
Creed nor calling
Distributing Godhead's aftermath

Nay . . . 'tis not

Was it the fear of Guilt?

Madness that eats at you
Fouling the years furthermore

Damn right!
'tis fear

Of surviving

Terry W. Sako
USMC (Retd), Vietnam Veteran

In the last chapter we looked at how PTSD can so disorientate a casualty that they lose their families and in many cases their homes. For many veterans this is just the beginning of the downward spiral to ruin. Rod is a veteran of the Falklands war, a member of the Parachute regiment. This is his story, in his own words. As such, some of the time he expresses himself with the blunt language and sincerity of a common soldier.

I was in the Falklands. I was there to do a job. I was airborne and knew I was one of the best trained on the islands. I remember one day we were taking on an Argie position....bunkers...all in a line, pathetic because they couldn't fire in support of each other, so we just took out each bunker one by one....we only came under fire from the bunker we were attacking at the time. It was a duck shoot really, shit.... we were shooting 16 and 17 year old conscripts....they didn't have a chance...not against us.

We entered the Argies defensive positions, we were still taking fire, small arms, grenades, mortars....and we were taking casualties, but we were like an unstoppable train as we moved forward. We didn't take any prisoners, we couldn't, they would have been a liability and would slow us down. So during the assault we just...we just shot them all. You've got to remember the adrenaline was pumping through our bodies, we were on a high and our training was well and truly kicking in, you don't even have time to think....it was shoot first or die. We killed everyone we came across.

A grenade went off in one of the Argie trenches and it just didn't sound nice... not nice at all...not like in the films...people were screaming in pure agony, some screaming for minutes, some for hours before they eventually died...it did my head in.

It was getting towards the end of the battle, it was starting to get light, the enemy were close, all around us I think. I had my 9mm pistol as well as my rifle, we all had pistols, just in case we got a jam on the SLR. The Argies weren't even human any more...they were just targets we had to take out. One guy came out from behind a hedge, I shot him with half a mag from my pistol, 6 maybe 7 rounds, all centre mass.....it was then I saw the white flag, it wasn't really a flag, just a dirty white rag. Was he trying to surrender? I don't know ... I really don't know but his face haunts me to this very day. He looked so surprised, pleading almost as the rounds ripped through his chest and I remember he looked like my kid brother ... he looked like my kid brother who was still at school.

After the war we came back home to a country that had absolutely no idea how crap it had been and most of us didn't want to talk about what happened out there because the people asking just didn't understand. They saw the neat pictures on the telly, but they never saw the shit we saw, or experienced anything we went through. Not long after I got back the dreams started, terrible dreams, nightmares ... of the young kids I had shot ... of the young soldiers with ... with bits of their bodies missing after a grenade or mortar round exploded amongst them, it all seemed so real at times, the dreams ... so real. I started drinking to help me get to sleep, at first it helped but then the dreams returned. I was jumpy as hell, can you imagine that ... there was I, airborne, a war vet, scared shitless of loud noises. It was fucking embarrassing. I also started to feel guilty, I lost a few mates in the Falklands ... and I wondered why I had survived, what made me so special, I felt I hadn't done enough.

I was discharged a year after I had received my medal, I was a wreck, the MO said I was an alcoholic, and that I was 'a little depressed'. I went to the funerals of 5 of my mates; of course I was a little fucking depressed! I kept my emotions bottled up, but soon the bottle was full, then it was overflowing. My wife left me ... she left me ... taking our daughter, she said I was ... shit ... she said I was too dangerous to live around, too violent ... get that ... too violent. I let her go ... I had to ... I was in tears as I watched them drive away in the taxi; it was the last time I ever saw them.

Then I lost my family after I beat up my kid brother. I went round to my parents' house one night, I was pissed as hell, full of booze and I collapsed on the front lawn, Joe my kid brother, came out to help me but all I saw was the Argie I shot in the chest, I lost the plot, I attacked him and ... and ... I almost killed him. My dad pulled me off then told me to leave ... for good ... I was gutted ... I wasn't even allowed to see him at the hospital.

I couldn't keep any job, even poxy jobs like security guard or warehouseman. I was a mess, and anyone I asked for help just turned their backs on me. I couldn't afford the rent on the flat I was in, I was spending all my money on booze, I became homeless and lived on the streets. I lasted 3 months before I tried taking my own life ... the first time I jumped off a bridge but survived ... the irony ... it was probably my training that saved me, maybe I instinctively did a Para roll as I landed ... fuck knows ... but I survived with little more than a sprained ankle.

The intrusive thoughts, flashbacks and dreams were getting worse. I beat up a homeless man one night ... just ... just because he was wearing an American issue combat jacket. I heard he spent 6 weeks in intensive care. I ... I tried to hang myself but someone saved me, someone was trying to tell me that I wasn't meant to die, but I tried twice more. The last time I tried I was saved by a Good Samaritan, I was that pissed off I beat him to a pulp, I was so angry with him ... he died in hospital a week later. I was charged and convicted of murder.

In prison the prison psychiatrists are useless, a bunch of 3rd rate failures who no-one else would employ, idiots the lot of them and they have no idea what's wrong with me, or don't care. Do they listen to me when I tell them what is going on in my head? What I went through? NO, not one little bit, they just see me as a prisoner, as a murderer. I didn't mean to kill the man, I lost the plot, but I got a life sentence for it. I was ordered to kill teenagers in the Falklands and I did, with lethal efficiency and they called me a hero, gave me a fucking medal. I fought for Queen and Country, for the people on the Falklands, and now that I need a bit of help, where are they, where is the army, what happened to 'we're all one big family', where is my country now I am in need of help?

Rod's pre-trial psychiatric examination said there was nothing wrong with him, the examination lasted 25 minutes. Subsequent prison psychologists and psychiatrists said he was suffering from mild depression and withdrawal symptoms from alcohol. Rod has since been examined by two independent psychiatrists of some standing; both have independently diagnosed chronic PTSD, brought on by his experiences in the Falklands. The prison, courts and the MoD have chosen to ignore the reports written by the two prominent psychiatrists.

Rod's story is a classic example of the way PTSD manifests among our veterans. The intense, first hand horrors of war. The return home and sense of alienation. The intrusive memories, flashbacks and nightmares. Attempts to self-medicate with alcohol and drugs. Hyper-vigilance and over-reaction to any startling event. Wild emotional swings from total shutdown to violent outbursts. Alienation and loss of family due to alcohol and violent rage. Inability to hold down even the most mundane of jobs. Homelessness, suicidal tendencies, violent attacks while under the influence of alcohol, drugs or as the result of a flashback and ultimately imprisonment. Rod is just one of thousands of prison inmates who are British veterans.

What is even more telling is that according to the National Ex-Services Association as many as 7% of the total prison population in the UK is made up of veterans. And given that our prison population has just passed 80,000, that means as many as 5,600 inmates could be veterans. If we take the conservative 9% figure for the rate of PTSD then 504 prisoners are incarcerated because of their medical condition. A similarly conservative estimate for keeping someone in prison is £37,500 per annum. So when we do the numbers we find that the country spends almost £19 million every year to lock up British military veterans simply because these casualties cannot get effective diagnosis and treatment for their injury. If we assume that the average time in prison is three years, each PTSD casualty who has been incarcerated costs the country £112,500. That much money would pay for a significant amount of treatment, therapy and training to help these individuals once again become productive members of society – just as they were when they wore our country's military uniform with pride.

According to the SSAFA website (http://www.ssafa.org.uk/prisonServices.html):

In 2004, SSAFA Forces Help and The Royal British Legion joined Prison In-Reach. An MOD led forum created with the following aims in mind:

- *To show the range of services provided by veteran organisations*
- *To reduce re-offending amongst veterans*
- *To find out the number of ex-Service personnel in prison*
- *To find out the needs of the prisoner and their families before they are released*
- *To give immediate help to dependants of prisoners*

Two things are quite striking about this programme. First is that the MoD doesn't know how many veterans are incarcerated and needs to find out and second – no mention is made of providing support for the imprisoned veterans who are casualties of PTSD. If there is to be any serious attempt at reducing the number of our veterans who are incarcerated we need to address the root cause of at least 9% of these cases – the lack of effective treatment for PTSD among ex-service personnel.

In the next chapter, the last of our case studies, will look at how the veteran can expend so much energy trying to cope with the symptoms of his PTSD, how hard they fight to do the right thing and protect those around them and finally how they react when they run out of the personal resources to keep fighting.

CHAPTER 7

ESCAPING THE PAIN

By
David Walters

RIOT

Petrol bombs being hurled through the air
The banging of dustbin lids also blare!
Scan the windows for snipers too,
Danger is upon us, and we are too few …

People acting like animals crazed with rage,
They turn upon the soldiers in a rampage.
Seconds to decide if you live or die:
Deploy your men thereby!

Pulling the soldiers into a trap?
The sniper? The bomb? It could be a death trap!
Sanity? That's now gone.
Draw and use the baton-gun …

Pursue the enemy – it's him or you,
Terrorists? We don't know who is who.
Screams from women and children too.
Deadly threats it's all so true …

Protestants cheer – Catholics scream.
Tell me "Was this all a dream?"
Scenes of destruction with blood and gore,
Doppelgangers became the images of war!

Jimmy Johnson

Simon was born on Tyneside and moved to the Midlands as a young child. He had always been fascinated by the military and joined the Army as a junior leader immediately on leaving school.

He joined the Royal Artillery Air Defence Regiment in 1979 and served until 1983. During this time he saw service in the Falklands Campaign. At only 19 years old, he was in command of an air defence unit stationed on the Falklands Islands. His unit was air lifted off the Sir Galahad to set up their air defence battery to protect the ships near Fitzroy.

On initial deployment of the air defence battery, they found that the tracking unit was not functional. While still trying to get the system to operate, Argentinean aircraft attacked the Sir Galahad and Sir Tristram. Galahad was hit and immediately started to burn. Simon ran to the radio station close to his unit and called for a casevac (casualty evacuation) then returned to his battery. They managed to get the tracking unit working when a second wave of Argentinean planes flew over. They hit one of the attacking planes.

The attack on Sir Galahad and Sir Tristram was the most lethal single event against British forces with approximately 50 deaths. According to analysis after the war, the effectiveness of short range air defence batteries in protecting from fast flying aircraft without the benefit of long range defences to protect from high flying aircraft was seriously flawed.

When working with PTSD casualties, guilt is a major issue which has to be resolved. In most cases the guilt the veteran feels is due to a perceived sense of failure. They let the side down. They didn't do the job they were trained to do. In virtually all cases the guilt is in no way attributable to any failure in their actions. The failures were usually due to equipment defects, poor intelligence, the confusion of war or simply time and chance.

But according to Simon, "I killed fifty people". And from this position of guilt, he decided that he had to do 50 years self-penance.

On returning to the UK, Simon's performance in the military rapidly deteriorated. Only six months after his Falklands experience he was dishonourably discharged for being "Absent Without Leave" (AWOL). Simon was a boxer in the army and prided himself on his physical fitness. After leaving the service he quickly turned to drink and roamed the streets for up to six months at a time.

Simon then had some good luck. He met a young woman, settled down and actually gained qualifications in telecommunications. During this period his daughter was born. He found that he was unable to hold down a job. His relationship with his girlfriend lasted 4 years but then broke down due to his aggression and he once again found himself roaming the streets. He never saw his daughter again after her second birthday.

During his time on the streets, his operated under his military conditioning. He was living rough but kept himself smart "no matter what" by washing in swimming pools and gyms. He didn't beg or steal and tried to maintain a sense of pride. He was simply following the survival techniques he had learned in the military. His condition worsened. Simon was regularly using alcohol to self-medicate against the hallucinations and voices he was regularly hearing in his head. The voices would command him to commit violent acts and he was imprisoned for the first time.

On being released from prison he began to self-harm. This included cutting, self-strangulation and causing fights so that he would be beaten to fulfil the requirements of his self-penance. His relationship with his family deteriorated and other than an occasional short phone call he had no contact with them for 21 years.

He continued to roam the country and was eventually admitted to a psychiatric hospital after his first suicide attempt. He stated the local moors reminded him of the Falklands. He was then removed from the mental hospital for attempting to kill another patient. He served six months in prison for GBH. During this time his cell mate attempted suicide by cutting his wrists. When he came to his senses he asked Simon for assistance. He refused and calmly watched his cellmate bleed to death without any sense of emotion or inclination to inform the guards what had occurred.

His release was followed by another period of homelessness after which he was taken in by a friend. Then he met another girl and settled down once again. He dried out, started to renovate a barn and even looked at setting himself up in business as a worm farmer. Simon had finally started to make some progress in his life.

Throughout this period he was starting to make his new relationship work. He was still seeing the faces of three soldiers who had died on Sir Galahad.

His combat gear would never leave his side and he was constantly encouraged to do violence by the voices in his head. When he listened to the radio he heard whispers calling his name and he felt that he was the subject of secret communications.

His situation took an unexpected turn after he got into an argument with the landlord of his local pub. He was banned from the pub and decided that he must kidnap, torture and kill the landlord. He dressed in his full combat gear, dug a hole to dispose of the body and made his preparations for executing revenge. His plan was intercepted by a friend who was able to defuse the situation. After this Simon was put in contact with a private facility specialising in veterans suffering from PTSD.

He described his mental state before the plan to murder the pub landlord as follows.

> *"Self penance for the death of 50 fellow soldiers killed on the Sir Galahad Falklands war 1982.*
>
> *Voices telling me to commit violent situations, also I see visions of the dead. Homelessness, i.e. living rough. Washing in swimming pools and gyms.*
>
> *Appearance always kept smart no matter what, no begging or stealing, pure survival techniques.*
>
> *Imprisonment, no affect, found to be a release from the streets.*
>
> *Self harm, mainly cutting, self strangulation, fighting etc.*
>
> *No financial sense.*
>
> *A term of self esteem going to university*
>
> *Living a double life, voices, visions.*
>
> *Daughter born – back to streets, first bail hostel, imprisonment.*
>
> *No family ties for 21 years except the odd phone call or visiting – of which proceeded to me leaving without notice. Family are strangers to me.*
>
> *Relationship breakdowns. Travel the country.*

> *Admitted to mental ward for attempted hanging.*
>
> *Removed to mental hospital for attempting to kill fellow patient.*
>
> *Imprisonment, after leaving hospital.*
>
> *Homelessness.*
>
> *Twin sister takes me in, met new partner.*
>
> *Voices still making me violent. Visions.*
>
> *Not much memory of situations. Return to area where I know peace best.*
>
> *Partner live in tent below mountain; military survival techniques 10 weeks. Move to caravan 1 year. Move into cottage visions worse, self harm continuing.*
>
> *Argument with local so I attempted to kidnap, torture and kill. Dressed in military combat kit in violent situations. Police would not arrest me.*
>
> *Accepted as patient (emergency). Partner could not cope.*
>
> *My combat will never leave my side, just in case. The enemy rules.*
>
> *Self penance for the death of the Galahad.*
>
> *1 year penance for each life lost.*
>
> *And "No" I do not feel sorry for myself. It is my penance".*

After Simon had spent some time in the veterans PTSD home he again described his condition.

> *"In a bad way from attempted kidnap.*
>
> *Self harming by scratching arms, no confidence, panic attacks.*
>
> *Voices, visions kept to myself until I could trust a particular member of staff.*
>
> *Being controlled by voices. Telling me to return to kidnap situation.*

Train hard for this possibility.

Being tugged from bed by visions. Three separate soldiers who may have died on the Galahad.

Keep combat kit for situations.

Lots and lots of counselling via staff and key worker and counsellor.

Voices and visions still returning but not nearly as bad.

Medication is working along with counselling and talking to the lads.

I keep fit now for exhaustion to keep visions voices away and because I enjoy the physical fitness mainly boxing.

I now have excellent support from staff, ex-partner – close friends.

I have a small worm farm. And about to begin a self build of stables. People are in support. Now contact my father by telephone."

After four months of counselling he had an improved outlook and was actually planning to live in a caravan while he converted a barn to live in. His violent outbursts subsided and he only had two episodes which resulted in his retiring to his room to destroy his personal property rather than get into confrontation with others.

Seven months after entering the home he was assessed as being fit for discharge. His anger was under control using medication and anger management. His panic attacks were still problematic but he was able to go out alone. The nightmares were controlled with medication and his visual hallucinations were under control although his voices were with him at all times.

Throughout his time in the private facility there was a constant battle to obtain funding to allow him to continue to stay there. The initial funding was obtained from the Army Benevolent society, later some funding was provided from his local NHS trust and for some of his time he was allowed to stay at the facility free of charge.

The following year, during the anniversary of the Falklands War, Simon became very unstable. He was anxious about being given a flat in a city as he had always tried to distance himself from others by staying in the country. The voices in his head were instructing him to kill someone. And is a desperate attempt to protect those around him, he tried several times to get arrested and locked up because his urge to kill was so intense. He was provided accommodation at the private facility but his local health authority refused to fund his stay and so he returned to his flat.

Less than one month later Simon phoned one of the veterans he knew in the area and told him that he was in trouble. The veteran went to see Simon and found him lying on his living room floor in a pool of blood. He had repeatedly slashed himself with his combat knife. An ambulance was called and Simon was admitted to the local hospital for emergency treatment.

Simon was later released and spent another period as a day patient at the private facility. On this occasion the local health authority did fund this treatment and Simon eventually returned into the community where he was able to cope for almost a whole year. He kept himself busy by redecorating his flat and in the words of his housing support officer *"always presented himself in a friendly and polite manner and I have found him to be a motivated and self-reliant person. He has turned his flat into a home by decorating it throughout, and I have seen 'professionals' do far worse jobs".*

Then the anniversary of the Falklands war came round again. Two weeks after he had received such a glowing commendation from his housing support officer his condition worsened and the voices in his head became stronger. In an attempt to protect those around him, Simon sent a series of texts to warn people to stay away.

19 APRIL:

1310 PLEASE TELL EVERYONE TO KEEP AWAY IT IS NOT SAFE. VOICES ARE DREADFUL.

1318 I'VE JUST HAD A RADIO CHECK FROM BRAVO, SEND MESSAGE, GONE TO TRENCH TO ZULU, NO OVERDOSE, PAPA MAY BE COMING BY LAND, IT IS NOT SAFE.

1642 WHY WOULD I NEED TO COME THERE. IVE BEEN ASLEEP ALL DAY, JUST WOKE UP WITH ME BOOTS ON. FOUND TXT ON FONE IN ARMY SIGNALS AND VOICEMAIL FROM BENNY RE SITREP. WHAT HAVE I DONE WRONG I AM WORRIED NOW.

1916 I FEEL THAT NOBODY AROUND ME IS GOING TO BE SAFE, NOT EVEN MY PARENTS AND FRIENDS. I AM GOING TO HAVE TO LIVE LIFE AS A RECLUSE. I KNO[W] I AM A DANGEROUS MAN, I DON'T WANT ANYONE TO GET HURT, JUST [W]ISH POLICE WOULD TAKE ME AWAY TO A SAFEHAVEN. I CANNOT BE TRUSTED ANYMORE, I HAVE LOCKED MYSELF IN IN CASE IT HAPPENS AGAIN.

1917 I WONT LET ANYONE IN UNLESS I AM HANDCUFFED, EVERYONE IS IN DANGER, ICARNT [sic] COPE ITS LIKE IM JEKYL AND HYDE, I AM SO SCARED.

20 APRIL:

0815 DON'T WORRY I HAVENT TAKEN THE OVADOSE WAY OUT I AM LOCKED IN MY FLAT THAT'S THE SAFEST WAY FOR ME TO MEET MANKIND, I DON'T WANT TO SEE ANYMORE HEAD DOCTORS. I HAVE SEEN PLENTY AND NONE CAN HELP. I AM DESTINED TO LIFE AS A RECLUSE, THEN GOD MAY FIND ME PEACE.

Simon took a drug overdose that afternoon and was found by another veteran who had become concerned as a result of the text messages he had received. Simon was taken to an acute medical ward and treated for his suicide attempt.

A week later he was referred to a consultant psychologist whom he had previously seen. Unfortunately his mistrust of civilian "head doctors" meant that he did not allow follow up by the psychiatrist or the community mental health team. He was offered an appointment for early May. The day before the appointment Simon phoned up to cancel. Because he missed the appointment the psychiatrist refused to approve funding for the private home, the one place that he had found safety and actually made any improvement. Simon was offered a substitute appointment for late June.

Five weeks after missing his May appointment Simon finally lost his battle with his voices from the Sir Galahad. He became another casualty of the 1982 Falklands War, killed by his own hand with a drug overdose of his prescription medication.

The sad story of this young 19-year-old soldier, his sense of guilt and remorse for failures way beyond his control, his 20 year battle to control his violent rage, his desperate attempts to get himself locked up so that he would not pose a threat to others, the inability of existing civilian resources to deal effectively with the unique needs of military PTSD casualties and the institutional bias against independent service providers who actually can make a difference is being played out in hundreds of lives today.

Simon was just one of many casualties in this story. He killed himself. But what of the pain and anguish caused to his first wife and their young daughter, to his cohabiting partner who stood by him for many years, his father, mother, brother and twin sister who tried repeatedly to reach out to him? The network of veterans who are themselves PTSD casualties who try and provide whatever ad hoc support they can to help each other. All of these people are just as much casualties of PTSD as Simon was.

For every veteran suffering from the brain injury PTSD, there are dozens of others whose lives are affected, often irreparably, sometimes fatally by the behaviour of each one of Britain's growing army of untreated PTSD casualties. In the following chapters we intend to provide some hope for the casualties of PTSD and their families.

CHAPTER 8

THE VETERAN RETURNS HOME

By
Jimmy Johnson

This chapter has been provided by Jimmy Johnson, a veteran soldier of Aden and Northern Ireland, who was "mentioned in dispatches" for his service in Northern Ireland. He has been diagnosed as suffering from complex (combat) Post Traumatic Stress Disorder (PTSD). Jimmy has written about his experiences over four decades as a PTSD casualty. His booklet "Veterans and their families – Survival guide to combat post traumatic stress disorder" is designed to give serving and ex-serving British Forces (and their families) an introduction into the effects and symptoms of PTSD. Only minor formatting and editorial changes to the original work have been conducted.

(Note – the condition Jimmy calls combat PTSD is now known as complex PTSD).

The Home Coming

Many British Armed Forces personnel who have served, or are still serving on tours of duty around the world will get exposed to traumatic incidents. A great majority of these Armed Forces personnel have not, or will not, be 'switched off' once their tour of duty is finished.

Some veterans will return to their families suffering from Combat PTSD and this will now become a problem for the veterans and their families. No-one has told the veterans' families that the veterans are only back home in body - not in mind. The families of returning veterans **MUST** be pre-warned about Combat PTSD and be alerted to watch their sons', or husbands' behavioural patterns on their return to normal peacetime conditions. Thousands of British Armed Forces families have already seen the ruination and break-up of their relationships because of the non-existent treatment by the MoD for Combat PTSD.

Veterans suffering from Combat PTSD, and not having been de-sensitised, have many, many pitfalls waiting for them on their return from conflict. Most veterans suffer in silence but many have whole repertoires, or entire stocks of traumatic incidents still locked in their minds. You could describe a veteran who has not been de-sensitised and suffering from PTSD on his return home to peacetime conditions as like a 'brick' which is thrown into a calm pool of water. The ripples, caused by the veterans conditions mainly affect the veteran's family and friends and people who come into direct contact with him, and all these people could become part of some disastrous repercussions by the veteran as he brings the war home.

However, the biggest problem facing the families of troops/veterans, apart from knowing their loved ones need psychological help, is getting their loved ones to realise there is something seriously wrong. PTSD 'masks' itself and the majority of troops/veterans do not know or realise they are suffering from this disorder; they just survive each day 'locked' in their war.

It is the families of troops/veterans who first recognise this change in behaviour of their loved ones. NOT the troops/veterans themselves.

So it is essential that troops/veterans and their families **need** to know about the problems of combat related PTSD, at least this will give them a chance to know or recognise the symptoms of this condition otherwise combat related PTSD will destroy and ruin the lives of troops/veterans and their families.

A veteran suffering combat related PTSD will probably have been cast adrift into "civvy street" and been left to cope with this disorder alone in ignorance.

Have you served and left the Armed Forces? Time since discharge makes no difference - PTSD does not have a time limit period. It does not miraculously disappear with age. Or are you back home after serving in Combat, Active/ Peacekeeping tours of duty? If yes, did you undergo or were put through a de-sensitisation programme and treated for combat related PTSD?

The veteran's behaviour at home begins to get on his wife's and family's nerves.

If, like many thousands of other troops/veterans you were left to cope alone you could be, or probably are, suffering from combat related PTSD.

If you do not admit making mistakes - you never learn from them.

Sadly troops/veterans suffering combat related PTSD will never learn from their mistakes, they will do the same things again and again especially when under pressure because they are still 'locked' in the war.

Basically, troops/veterans suffering from this disorder have had their whole 'psychological universe' (morals/behaviour/character) turned round and are unaware of this matter. In plain English since suffering from this disorder troops/veterans have been trying to put square pegs into round holes and need psychological help to turn this back round again.

Recognising Combat PTSD

Veterans will not tell their wives, families or friends that they are suffering from Combat PTSD - because they simply do not know themselves.

A veteran suffering Combat PTSD will be the last person in the world to admit or realise they are suffering from this disorder. The veteran himself will not know, or have any idea he has changed in character or in mannerisms - he still thinks himself as normal.

The problems that face a veteran suffering Combat PTSD and having to come to terms with it are horrifying. The greatest shock will probably be the loss of his wife and family - they will have tried their hardest to cope with the person they got back from the wars - but eventually even they will have given up in despair with the veteran.

The veteran will also realise that his whole life has been ruined since suffering this disorder; he would probably have had a good promising career in front of him - now nothing - his and his family's lives ruined.

The veterans families are the best placed to know and recognise the changes in their loved ones - not the veterans themselves.

Strange Behaviour at Home

Example: The veteran and his wife may be sat at home talking and the veteran's wife asks a question.

The veteran (for some strange reason) moves from where he is sitting and goes over to where his wife is sitting to answer the question. The veteran will then kneel down beside his wife just to answer her question and talk to her (at first his wife may think he's being romantic or something like that) but this behaviour does not stop, he keeps doing it and it gets on her nerves.

The veteran does not consciously know he is doing this strange behaviour, and it is not strange behaviour to the veteran. To the veteran this behaviour is normal; he regularly moved and spoke this way when out on 'operations' (Observation Posts/Ambush Sites) during his tour of duty. He automatically makes himself as small a target (from the windows) as possible and doesn't want to be heard speaking.

Example: The veteran's family have noticed he is out of the home each evening and/or early each morning.

The veteran will start making excuses to be out of the family home each evening and early morning. The reason for this is that he 'must' check the surrounding area outside his home evenings or early mornings. If the veteran doesn't do this he feels nervous or on edge. He may leave the home for an hour or more, sometimes he may just do a quick check - only a couple of minutes. Unknown to the veteran he is checking the surrounding area because he is going out on patrols.

He may get worse and start doing this behaviour every morning and every evening (when he gets like this he is under a lot of pressure and he is plunging deeper into Combat PTSD) he needs help quickly.

Jobs - Work

The veteran after a few weeks back home manages to get a job, then only after a few days or weeks later he packs the job in.

Example: A veteran working on a building site, a normal everyday building site.

A veteran suffering Combat PTSD does not know, or realise, that when he first arrives on the building site the first initial sights he sees in his mind are not those of a building site - he will get quick rapid 'flashes' of bombed out buildings. The sight of half finished buildings (rooftops, doors and windows missing) will register in his mind as bombed out buildings - he saw these bombed out buildings on his tour of duty. The 'flashes' he sees will only be for a second or so and then they will be gone. He won't take much notice of these flashes because they were that quick - in and out.

During the next few days or weeks, a lot depends on how much pressure the veteran is under at home and at work, and if the veteran is under a lot of pressure the flashes will come at him more often and for much longer periods - they can even bring fear to the veteran.

Example: The veteran gets a job driving a delivery van or something to do with driving a vehicle.

The nightmares the veteran suffers - usually the same one - can be kicked off or opened up in his mind by events or occurrences from during the day. These events or occurrences that trigger the nightmares consist of everyday matters such as arguments or worry. The main culprit though is television - TV News programmes - which broadcast many traumatic sights from around the world, sights of recent bombings and shootings, straight into the veteran's living room and mind.

Once the nightmares have been triggered by these daily events or occurrences the veteran will get a very disturbed sleep, he will only get one and a half to two and a half hours' sleep before he is shocked awake.

Communications and Family

The veteran suffering from Combat PTSD sits at home and hardly ever speaks to his wife and family.

Example: Communication between the veteran and his wife or family now seems to be non-existent.

At one time before his tour of duty the veteran was nearly always happy, laughing and joking, now nothing he sits there and hardly speaks. The veteran when he returned home could not speak to his wife and family about the horrors he saw or was involved in. He has to shut those horrors, traumatic incident, out of his family's lives, thinking he is protecting them from the horrors also. He was quite happy and content with that situation, by not speaking to them about those horrors they could not become involved and they were safe. But unknowingly to the veteran, by shutting his wife and family out of the traumatic incidents, his sub-conscious carried on protecting them. His sub-conscious knows the veteran still loves his wife and family so to protect them it carries on building up barriers, and eventually his wife and family will be shut out.

The veteran looks and sees his wife and family around him - like looking at them through a shop window - and they are 'safe' so he is happy.

Drinking & Drugs

The veteran suffering Combat PTSD starts drinking alcohol or taking drugs.

Example: The veteran's wife or family notice he is drinking alcohol heavily, they probably won't know about the drugs until it is too late.

The veteran will start drinking alcohol every night if he can. This is because after the horrors of being involved in the traumatic incidents it is the only way he feels he can cope or relax. In the veteran's mind just the thought of going to bed sober will haunt him, he wants to get drunk - he wants to get so drunk he passes out - the only way he knows how to forget the horrors.

The veteran will do anything to stop the nightmares. He is that afraid or scared of the nightmares. From the drinking he will try drugs - heaven - no dreams. No nightmares just a deep sleep. In the veteran's mind it's simple, if he doesn't drink or take drugs he doesn't sleep.

Got to be Alone

The veteran may have a good job and working as normal then suddenly he disappears, away from everyone.

Example: The veteran suddenly disappears; he doesn't turn up for work or at home. He may go missing for a few hours or a few days or even a few weeks.

The veteran gets a build-up of pressure, the sound of cars backfiring, the housing estate he lives on, women or children screaming or shouting (whilst playing), people he know and loves. Even at times his own wife or children can become the victims involved in the traumatic incidents he was involved in, his wife won't see love in his eyes - only horror.

All these factors contribute to a build-up of pressure in the veteran's mind, everyone and everything around him. He has got to get away; he's got to be alone so he disappears.

The veteran will disappear to a 'safe place' only he knows; time will mean nothing to him. This safe place is where he knows he can be alone and feel safe. He will be able to see all the surrounding area and no-one will be able to approach him without being seen. If anyone approaches him or comes near his position, he will move away without being seen, he was used to living like this on his tour of duty on operations.

When the veteran comes back to normality he will turn up back in the real world again, as if nothing is wrong, as if people haven't missed him or he hasn't been anywhere. If people ask him where he has been he will say anything that comes into his head, he doesn't know. The reason why he doesn't know where he's been is because he flipped in and flipped out of a flashback.

Wrong Information

The veteran suffering from Combat PTSD will at times feel very nervous for no apparent reason.

Example: The veteran will have this nervous feeling from the moment he wakes in the morning. In reality there is nothing for the veteran to feel nervous about but for some reason he does.

When the veteran is feeling anxious or nervous he goes on a different track of thought than normal people. He becomes hyper vigilant, he sees things other people don't see.

The veteran goes out shopping with his wife and as they come out of his home they see the next-door neighbour's curtains move. To the veteran's wife and normal people this movement of the curtains means the next-door neighbours are up and about; to the veteran this movement of the curtains could mean a threat. He will automatically start checking all the surrounding rooftops, windows or anywhere a sniper could be hiding, which puts him on a different track of thought to everyone else. Again when the veteran has this nervous feeling, anything can set his mind off on different thoughts.

His own wife or family, they could be at the front door of their home wanting to be let in or they could be trying to call the veteran on the telephone. When the veteran is like this he will ignore his wife and family at the door, he may even try to hide from them. He won't answer the telephone; he will ignore it until it stops ringing. When he is like this even his own wife and family do not register in his mind, even they become threats.

The veteran 'automatically' gets this wrong information fed to him, yet to him this information is very real.

Sounds & Noises

The veteran feels threatened if he hears sounds or noises he cannot recognise (especially at home).

Example: The veteran goes on 'alert', his heart will seem to beat faster when he hears strange sounds or different noises. He automatically picks up different background noises without realising he's picking them up.

The veteran is always alert and listening for different sounds and noises. Once he knows the sound or noise is no threat to him he calms down - until the next sound or noise.

Sometimes the veteran picks up background noise without realising he's picking them up. The veteran could be sat at home watching the television - checking the football results? There could be background noises i.e. fireworks display. The fireworks display, small bangs or explosions, may not at first register with the veteran but unknowingly the veteran is picking these small bangs or explosions up and the veteran's train of thought will start to move away from the football results.

The veteran will have flashes of when he was chasing after gunmen or of something of that nature. These flashes are opening the door in the veteran's mind, back to his tour of duty. The veteran may just shrug these flashes out of his mind and get back to watching the football results on the television. The veteran will then start to have flashes of his worst traumatic incident - the horror. He may again try to shrug these flashbacks out of his mind, which will be very hard to do - these flashbacks are much stronger than the opening flashes.

If somehow he manages to get these flashbacks out of his mind within seconds he will get even stronger flashbacks and he won't be able to ignore these. These flashbacks will be that strong they will take over his mind; this is all he will be seeing. The veteran's wife or family may see him holding his head trying to stop the flashbacks coming at him.

So whilst the veteran is still switched on he can be brought from watching football results back to the worst nightmare of his life, without even knowing why or how.

Panic

A veteran will not stay inside a small room when other strangers are present - he will leave.

Example: Some veterans do not feel safe when inside a small room with strangers, they may even panic.

A veteran may start to panic when inside a small room with 3 or more people, people the veteran does not know or trust. At first the veteran will feel on edge and may go on the offensive - by raising his voice. He will also make a beeline for the nearest door - his escape route - and leave the room. If for some reason he can't leave the room he may go into further panic, he will start to tremble and won't be able to breathe properly, he may even go into a trance or a coma.

Example: Sometimes a veteran may find himself outside a building, office block or factory, when he only remembers being inside the building.

The veteran could be surprised whilst inside a building, a noise, the sight or smell of something. The veteran's mind can then be triggered back to a threatening situation - bomb scare - he had inside a building on his tour of duty. The threat of a bomb inside a building, the veteran's job would be to clear the building. The veteran would have to check each room for people or suspect packages whilst moving through the building. Time would seem to speed up but his own movements would seem very slow. The veteran's mind would also be screaming at him telling him to run and save himself like everyone else, but duty or discipline is preventing him.

This time when the veteran gets surprised and the flashbacks are triggered, the flashback makes this building look exactly like the building he had cleared for real. The veteran may crack - enough is enough - and find himself running through the building, he won't be able to stop himself running, fear has taken over. This time the veteran has to escape, he will eventually find himself outside the building at a safe distance and wondering why he is outside the building.

Violence, Rage & Anger

The veteran has terrible outbursts of rage and resorts to violence easily. He wasn't like this before his tour of duty.

Example: The veteran explodes with rage at small trivial things. The rage explodes into fury and violence is used. The veteran may well end up in prison.

During his tour of duty the veteran would have been subjected to a daily routine of brutality directed at him each time he went on patrol. The veteran would receive verbal abuse, bricks and bottles, sometimes petrol or pipe bombs being thrown at him each day. Apart from that the veteran had other problems to deal with such as Gunmen, Snipers - he may have seen some of his mates shot dead. He could also have been involved in bombing incidents, seeing his mates and civilians being blown to pieces in front of him.

The MoD and Politicians, people who have never even had a brick thrown at them in anger in their lives, actually believe or think that British Armed Forces can have this violence/savagery thrown at them each day for months on end, and it does not affect them. The MoD and Politicians are terribly wrong if they believe this, or they are knowingly betraying their own Armed Forces. The truth is that the veterans often bring this violence back home - the high number of veterans inside the prison system can vouch for this.

Mood Swings & Depression

The veteran has very bad mood swings and suffers from bouts of depression and thoughts of suicide.

He could have been involved in dealing with rioting crowds of people, hand to hand fighting, people using axes, hammers, clubs or anything to kill him. The only way out of these life and death situations would be to use violence. Violence would be the only way to save himself and his men. Violence or force was part and parcel of life for the veteran.

Example: The veteran will at times get so down he really wishes himself dead.

The veteran will suffer problems of depression that will plunge him into thoughts of suicide, which will come at him repeatedly throughout the year. Some of the main factors that play a part in plunging the veteran into these mood swings are:

- Flashbacks - the veteran will get regular flashbacks of the main traumatic incident. The flashbacks will remind the veteran of the people that died and he survived.
- The veteran will also get these mood swings because of the people around him, wife, family or friends; they can also remind the veteran and look like the victims in the traumatic incident.
- And again, television - News programmes broadcasting recent terrorist attacks from around the world into the veteran's living room - and mind.

The worst and most harmful and vulnerable times for the veteran, when the veteran feels like a fish out of water and can't see himself living much longer, are the weeks leading up to and after his own traumatic incident - the anniversary.

Household Problems

The veteran does not seem to care or worry about the running of the family home, he doesn't seem interested.

Example: The veteran's wife or family have noticed that normal, everyday household problems do not seem to concern the veteran anymore; he seems to duck away from these problems.

The veteran's wife or family have noticed the veteran only seems to worry about things he shouldn't even worry about - keeping the curtains closed, strangers at the front door, only small trivial things. Yet the things that he should be worrying about - being evicted from their home, he doesn't seem to worry about. The veteran may not seem to care about these household problems, but he does worry about them very much. The problem with the veteran is he can't come up with a solution to any of these household problems; he only comes up with solutions or answers to a threat or violent situations.

When a veteran suffering from Combat PTSD worries or comes under pressure with problems at home, his mind only flips back to life or death situations - he dealt with these problems okay on his tour of duty.

The veteran becomes very vulnerable to a flashback situation, screams or shouts of women and children can flash the veteran back to rioting crowds, crowds of people who wanted the veteran dead, so normal household problems become life and death problems to the veteran. The veteran cannot handle normal household problems, he seems to have a hidden gear that comes into play when he is under pressure - pressure is the clutch.

Counselling Veterans

A veteran recognises straight away if the person counselling him knows anything about the horrors of war.

Example: When a veteran recognises that the person counselling him, psychiatrists/psychologists know nothing about the horrors of war, he automatically puts the barriers up and skips over the real problems, they haven't been there so he doesn't let them in.

Psychiatrists and psychologists have firstly got to get the veteran's trust before he will even think of letting them help him. Combat PTSD is like a bomb to him and he won't let anyone touch it until he knows they can deal with it. The veteran is very fearful of Combat PTSD, especially if he has already had reactions to it.

When the veteran decides to come out of the dark tunnel he has been hiding in and wants help with Combat PTSD he will experience certain happenings to himself. Talking to psychiatrists/psychologists about his traumatic incidents can set off certain reactions for the veteran. He may get one reaction in which he will start to get a very strong trembling/shaking feeling that will seem to start at the tips of his toes and then travels through his entire body. He may panic when this happens and he may start to skip over telling what truly happened.

Another reaction the veteran may have is when being questioned about his experiences of his tour of duty he will probably get very annoyed - annoyed at the ignorant questions being asked him. The questions and being annoyed may start another reaction. This reaction will start by him seeing scenes or flashes that come into his mind of his tour of duty. These scenes or flashes of his tour of duty will be like watching a film or video: the scenes or flashes will start to show the veteran a film of his tour of duty. The film will start to speed up, faster and faster like fast forwarding a video tape and then these scenes and flashes eventually run out like a film running off its reel.

The veteran will then see a black hole and he will start to feel as if he is being sucked into this black hole into nothingness. This black hole feeling lasts a few moments then the veteran comes back to normality **terrified**. Somehow the veteran has got to realise that the flashbacks are not real - **not real - NOT REAL**.

This chapter has provided an excellent insight into the problems that will be experienced by family members of the PTSD casualty. And these are the first hand experiences of a real casualty of PTSD. What adds even more poignancy to this section is the fact that Jimmy is serving a life sentence for committing two murders since leaving the British Army.

In the next chapter we will explore a unique, new method which had shown remarkable success in its initial testing for resolving long standing complex PTSD symptoms, such as nightmares, flashbacks, emotional withdrawal, suicidal tendencies and hypersensitivity/avoidance behaviour.

Jimmy Johnson suffered a flashback in 1974 which resulted in him clubbing a security guard to death. He was sentenced to prison and paroled after 9 years. 14 months later, only two weeks after his best friend in the army was killed in a car bomb, he suffered another flashback and beat his co-worker to death. He was sentenced to life imprisonment to serve a minimum of 20 years in prison. In 1994 a psychiatric report stated that he had worked through many of the psychological phenomena and the risk of re-offending was significantly reduced. In 2004 a report stated that he was a "model inmate" suffering from PTSD and that if he were to be released into the community the psychiatric support he receives would have to continue. Jimmy Johnson is still in prison.

Jimmy can be contacted through www.vetsinprison.org.uk.

CHAPTER 9

THE WALTERS METHOD™

By
David Walters

As a result of a long period of working with a wide variety of individuals operating in high intensity situations – torpedo operators in submarines, emergency responders in the nuclear power industry, emergency managers in local government and executive teams in multinational corporations – I realised that the way we train these people to operate in emergency situations is often flawed. The military method of drill, drill and drill again until it becomes an automatic response cannot easily be translated into the civilian or business community because there is just not the time available to repeat the training enough times for it to become an instinctive response. And there is valid debate whether an instinctive response, by rote, is appropriate to the complexity of a large organisation working its way through a corporate crisis while under public and governmental scrutiny.

So this led me to research stress and in particular stress in first responders – such as police, fire and ambulance crews. As a result of this research I learned numerous stress reduction techniques. Some were just totally flaky! Some were mainstream and effective, others not so. There are a variety of new techniques which have been used to counter PTSD, most notably Cognitive Behaviour Therapy (CBT) and Eye Motion Desensitisation and Reprogramming (EMDR). Both of these techniques have reported success with treating PTSD. But there is ongoing debate about the long term efficacy of these procedures, the length of time it takes to achieve results and the degree of abreaction they cause in the PTSD casualties.

So we have adopted a unique approach to helping these veterans who are casualties of PTSD. Before becoming casualties the majority of these service personnel were dynamic, self-directed, independent people fully capable of managing their own lives. So this programme has been developed to avoid the conflict these men have trying to explain themselves to civilians who do not understand their situation. Rather it is intended to teach them a variety of effective techniques in a safe and supportive environment so that they can once again achieve control over their own lives. The first time a veteran experiences these techniques they are extremely sceptical, hesitant about the effectiveness of the technique and to some degree afraid of re-traumatising themselves. So the initial training is conducted with a high level of individual coaching and support to help the veteran obtain quick and noticeable results. Once the veterans have gained confidence in the techniques they have learned, the programme focuses more on coaching support to encourage them to stay with the programme and deal with any secondary issues which may emerge.

The Training Programme

The Walters Method ™ has been developed against 3 fundamental principles:

- It should be easy to learn and self administer
- It should be easy to deliver, even over the phone
- It should not cause the casualty any additional pain

So based on these three fundamentals, we next addressed the most common problems for dealing with complex PTSD. These are:

- Re-traumatisation – which runs the risk of destabilising the casualty – even to the point of suicide
- Communicating core issues in a non-threatening way
- Effectively releasing the negative memory/emotion
- Identifying deep-rooted secondary issues
- Obtaining closure
- Supporting a credible vision of the future

Now to look at the tools we had to work with. During my research into stress resilience I identified a number of complementary techniques which could be applied to this situation. These included such things as Trauma Release Technique (TRT) - my own derivative of the Emotional Freedom Technique, Neuro Linguistic Programming, the Sedona Method, Tapas Acupressure Technique (TAT), aromatherapy, part therapy, brainwave entrainment, Terminal Release Communications (TRC), autogenic relaxation, life mapping, visualisation, goal setting and path working. None of these techniques in isolation held all the answers but presented together, sequentially, or in combination has produced remarkable results. The techniques are integrated into a seamless process and taught to the PTSD casualties during the initial training phase.

Over time we have developed and refined this protocol to the point where it now is. There are always new discoveries, or better ways of presenting or delivering the training and as these come along we will be very quick to test them, see how they can improve the protocol and then, if they add value to what we do, we will adopt them.

The protocol is delivered in two phases. The first, the intervention phase, starts with an intensive 3-day residential programme (afternoon, full day and morning). The purpose of this is to teach the trainee how to collapse their core issue as quickly and safely as possible and release the associated emotions surrounding the issue. Almost invariably these include anger, guilt, shame and sadness (often in that order). Also during the residential training the casualty is given a variety of techniques to improve their sleep. Once the initial release has been achieved many people say they feel there is something missing in their head. So we quickly work to create a positive future vision, set some goals and establish a support network to help the person make the transition from PTSD casualty to functional human being.

It is common for PTSD casualties to express no hope for their future, even a physical inability to think more than one day at a time. One casualty, who had constant thoughts of suicide, and had actually three unsuccessful attempts to his name, told us he had only one rule to live by. His rule number 1 was wake up alive tomorrow, rule number 2 was - see rule 1. It is always extremely distressing to hear how many of these veterans think about and plan their own death. In some cases they repeat these thoughts on a daily or hourly basis. Many more engage in irresponsible behaviour such as high speed, reckless driving or even commit self-harm. So creating a credible, coherent vision for the future and providing the support the casualty needs to make that transition is an important consideration of this training.

From experience, over 50% of people attending the course find secondary issues emerge after they have completed the initial residential training. Usually this happens within the first seven days after the initial one to one coaching. So a series of follow on calls are made by the training team to monitor the progress of the recovering veteran. These are a short telephone call to establish the well being of the veteran. If any issues are reported follow on telephone coaching is arranged. In virtually all cases this is sufficient to address the problem. This coaching support is provided for the first four weeks after the residential course.

Once this is completed the level of support is reduced to fortnightly calls in the second and third month and eventually monthly calls for the next three months. When other support agencies are engaged, it is intended to hand off the long term care to a suitably trained counsellor or field worker. This will free the training team to stay focussed on the critical initial four week period of the programme. The handover will be conducted at a three-way meeting with the veteran, a member of the training team and the field worker.

A significant concern at the beginning of the programme is that of re-sensitising and losing a casualty before they have had the benefit of learning the techniques. So even before someone is loaded onto the course there is a screening process. Although complex PTSD always has some form of co-morbidity or secondary personality disorder we insist that casualties coming on training are free from alcohol dependence and drug abuse for at least six months. We also require that they have been independently diagnosed with PTSD. This is a training programme to teach PTSD casualties a series of tools and techniques to help them overcome the symptoms of PTSD. So we need to be sure that the person is actually suffering from PTSD and not some other mental health issue which is outside the scope of this work. The final pre-requisite for joining the course is that the casualty must self refer. Many casualties are in denial, some are riddled with guilt and feel that they do not deserve to be released from their symptoms and many others are suppressing the core issues about their injury. These cases do not respond as well to the training as a casualty who has come to the realisation that they need help and are willing to make the commitment to do whatever it takes to obtain release from their PTSD symptoms.

Typically the residential training is run over three days. The course starts after lunch and all of the first day is spent on group activities. Once the joining routine is complete the casualties come together to learn the first, and extremely important defensive technique, the anchor.

The first part of the initial intervention consists of creating a multi-sensory anchor which can be used any time a trainee experiences extreme intensity from their memories. This is followed by creating a life map, which provides a very non-threatening visual expression of their life and trauma and gives an opportunity to identify primary and secondary issues which need to be addressed. The final session teaches the casualties the tools that will be used during the intervention sessions. The evening is given over to informal conversations and building rapport. No sleep aids are provided for the first night.

After breakfast an assessment of sleeping patterns is conducted and then the second day of the course is taken up with a series of one-to-one intensive interventions. Typically these take two hours which limits the course load to a maximum if four for each trainer. When the trainees are not involved with the intervention they are given time to experience a variety of support tools including autogenic relaxation, brainwave entrainment and bio feedback. Also, delegates are encouraged to keep working on their life maps, monitoring the progress they have made and keep collapsing any residual issues or emotions as they emerge.

An intervention starts by reviewing the life map and clearly identifying the primary and secondary issues which need to be addressed. Every precaution is taken to make sure that issues are collapsed as gently as possible. I don't believe there is any requirement to re-expose or re-traumatise the trainee so we conduct a "slow approach" to the issue. This starts by visualising a plain white envelope held at arms length and finishes when the trainee can create a mental movie of their trauma and play the movie without any anxiety, emotion or pain. At each step of the way the trainee is asked to identify their SUDS (Subjective Unit of Disturbance or Stress) score on a scale of 0 – 10. Whenever a score of 3 or higher is experienced we conduct a round of the Trauma Release technique (TRT) to collapse the intensity to a 1 or 0. Initially several rounds of TRT may be required, but as the intervention proceeds one or two rounds are enough.

When the trainee states that they are ready to produce their mental movie we conduct a visualisation technique called "the emotional throttle valve" (ETV) which allows the trainee to reduce their own emotional response and take total control of their emotional well being. Once the ETV has been set to zero they produce the movie. The trainee is asked to visualise a control panel consisting of 5 sliders, 3 buttons and a digital meter. The sliders represent taste, touch, smell, sound and colour. All of these are set to zero before creating the movie. The three buttons are play, stop and rewind and are used for playing the movie. The digital meter represents the SUDS score and the rule is made that the trainee must stop the movie the instant the meter reads 3 or higher.

The trainee then creates a black and white, silent movie from the position of the movie director i.e. an outside observer, not a participating actor. Once the movie is created the trainee gives it a title and we then play the movie. As soon as the digital meter hits 3 the movie stops and we conduct a round of TRT for the issue which was identified as the cause of anxiety. The movie is then rewound and the procedure continued until the entire movie can be observed without any idea causing a SUDS of 3 or more. Once this is achieved the trainee is invited to modify the sliders to a position which they are comfortable with and the process is repeated. This continues until the movie can be seen, from the observer position, with all sliders at 100% and a SUDS no higher than 3.

The process is now repeated with the trainee visualising themselves as an actor actually participating in the experience. Again the SUDS rule of 3 is invoked and TRT applied until the whole movie can be experienced without anxiety. Once this is achieved the trainee is invited to return to the ETV and open it up to a position which they are comfortable with. I normally suggest only 10% open for the first run through. The full sensory, experiential movie is then repeated and TRT applied as necessary. This process repeats until the trainee is able to re-experience the primary issue, with full emotional involvement and full sensory awareness and no accompanying anxiety. A good indicator that the trainee has finished the process are words like "I'm bored with this – do I have to do it again" or "shit happens – I need to get on with my life".

Once the primary issue has been collapsed, in the case of veterans, four emotions are very quickly experienced often in the following order – anger typically at the government, their unit and/or their mates for the sense of abandonment they felt. This is quickly collapsed with more TRT. Immediately after anger, the trainee experiences a sense of guilt – for not protecting/saving their mates or civilians, for living when another person died (possibly perceived as in their place), or for letting down the lads who still have PTSD and have not received help. Again TRT collapses this very quickly.

The final two emotions are shame and sadness. These are more nebulous than anger and guilt and so we have found they are not as easy to deal with using TRT because it is often difficult to identify a specific issue. In this case we use a combination of TAT and the Sedona method. This technique quickly dissolves any residual sense of shame or sadness.

The final step in the initial intervention is to identify whether the trainee has any incomplete or unresolved communications. These can be with individuals or groups who are living or dead, or even a third party who the trainees feels they need to communicate with. If required, the TRC procedure is conducted. The trainee is brought to a safe, relaxed state and then guided to a place in their head called the waiting room. When they are ready they enter the room and communicate with whoever they find there. In some cases there is no one and nothing is said, in others simple statements are declared and in the final group dialogues are conducted.

After this the life map is reviewed and any secondary issues which begin to emerge are identified for future work. If the secondary issue is causing immediate intensity then an intervention is started immediately.

At the end of the intervention day everyone, especially the trainer, is tired and typically after a brief chat and selection of sleep aid, everyone takes an early night.

On the morning of the third day the sleep quality of the trainees is assessed. The most commonly heard comment is "Wow – I haven't slept through the night like that in years" or "the demons have gone" or in one case "Damn, I've overslept and missed breakfast!"

After this we spend time reviewing and revising the life map and for many trainees suffering from chronic PTSD this is the first time since they developed PTSD that they have been able to look to the future. Once the trainee has come to terms with the idea that he actually has a future to look forward to we start the goal setting process. Trainees are encouraged to identify what they want to be, do or have in the seven key areas of their life – physical, emotional, relational, mental, spiritual, professional and financial. They are also asked to identify their event horizon, how far ahead they can envision their future. We then spend time creating an empowering vision statement which is both attractive and inspiring.

So far we have been successful in collapsing most or all symptoms of long term, late onset, complex PTSD in over 70% of all cases. Here are the words of some of those veterans who have helped us bring this programme to the level it is today:

I served in the Falklands as a corporal in 2 Para and was diagnosed with PTSD in 1993. Two weeks ago I had a major relapse. I was suicidal and all my memories came flooding back. I couldn't cope with them. Having done the course my head feels empty. All thoughts and memories I had are completely shredded and I'm sleeping straight through the night which is something I have not done for 25 years. Go in to this training with an open mind. Accept everything that you're being asked to do because it really does work.

Les Standish, Cpl 2 Para (Retd)

I spent 13 & half yrs in the Royal Army Medical Corps from '78 - '91, ret'd as Sgt. In Dec 2005 I was diagnosed by an ex-forces consultant psychiatrist as having severe chronic complex PTSD. I would not believe it so ended up being sectioned again and eventually saw yet another very highly qualified ex-services cons psych who yet again confirmed the original diagnosis. Since '82 I have been down the "Normal" route of failed treatments, therapies, therapists, NHS cpn's & so called specialists. My symptoms included intrusive thoughts, flashbacks, nightmares, hyper vigilance, paranoia, major anger, major fears, just to name a few.

On the Wed afternoon I was doing some relaxation techniques when I closed my eyes for the first time in 25yrs without my monsters and visions being there. Wed. night I had the first night's sleep over 3hrs in 25yrs with NO NIGHTMARES, WAKING UP AND ENDING UP PATROLLING THE GROUNDS AND SEARCHING FOR THE ENEMY & ANYTHING ELSE I USED TO DO IN MY SLEEP. Since Dec '82 I regularly saw the heads of dead people on the bodies of ordinary people in the street. After the Wed on the course I haven't seen any.

Like I said, I don't know how this program works, nor do I care how it works. All I can say at this point is that I am SYMPTOM FREE to date.

Steve "Taffy" Horvath, RAMC Sgt (Retd)

I am a former IEDD [Bomb Disposal] Warrant Officer and I was diagnosed with PTSD in 1999 following a series of traumas during the nineties. I was discharged from the British Army in 2001. My PTSD was initially diagnosed and treated at Haslar [military hospital] then I had no assistance until now. Over the last 10 years I have continued to experience the devastating impact of PTSD. This has resulted in 3 failed relationships and a constant living hell from nightmares, flashbacks and emotional shutdown. The procedures taught me by David Walters have given me a reason to live again. His techniques and easy going way of addressing issues has turned it around for me in just 2 telephone sessions. I am now living and working in Dubai and have felt so alone and isolated for so long. This is no longer the case.

Andy Haslam QGM, WO2 (Retd)

I joined the RAF in 1980 and in 1982, whilst working on bomb disposal, I was involved in an accident on a bombing range in Scotland. I was a member of a four man team, two of which were killed. One outright and the other later in hospital. I did manage to help save the life of one of my colleagues but continued to feel guilty that I couldn't have saved the one that later died too. I was only 19 years old and the medics said I would get over it.

I later went on to serve in the Gulf War in 1991. Because of time served I was discharged in 1992 but my ill health continued to dog me, flashbacks, nightmares and panic attacks. I had a break down in 2000 and several spells in hospital with stomach pains plus I was drinking heavily. In 2001 I went to the Gulf War Veterans Assessment unit in St. Thomas's in London where I was diagnosed with PTSD. I have had EMDR with a psychologist and spent time with Combat Stress in Shropshire, in 2006 - none of which had any lasting effect. I was admitted to hospital four times in twelve weeks with pancreatitis each time getting slowly worse. I went into rehab in December and have been dry ever since.

I was lucky enough to gain a place on a course with David Walters earlier this year and since then I have had no return of any of my symptoms and feel so much more confident. I am now looking forward to the future with my wife and family.

Howard Wesley, RAF Armourer (Retd)

I enlisted into the army aged 15 into the junior parachute coy. Passed my selection for Para training and was posted to 1 Para when the troubles started in 69. I was 17 and 5 months. I did a 4 month tour then went back in 70 until 72 I was present for the Abercorn bomb in Belfast where 32 were killed. I was on the streets during Internment for 8 days without going back to camp. I was at Bloody Sunday. Nothing bothered me. I also went back on op motorman and stayed another 4 months. I also served with the UN in Cyprus and in Berlin for 2 years.

When I was discharged from the regular army I had suffered anxiety symptoms. The cause was worry about leaving the army. When I left the regs I enlisted into the parachute regiment TA and served for 14 years. I suffered intermittently from anxiety/depression but finally left in 1990. I have had acupuncture, reflexology and been given plenty of tablets to take from my GP.

But I attended a PTSD course run by David Walters. Since this training I remain positive and have been given ways of dealing with my symptoms. I will continue with all the help and support I was given.

Phil King, WO2 (Retd)

During the Falklands I was caught in the attack on Sir Galahad. Physically I received only minor injuries but after I left the army the effects of my PTSD started to show. I ended up divorced because of my anger and violent outburst. I started to use alcohol to take away the pain and then I moved on to drugs. Eventually I made my first suicide attempt. Then I was put in contact with Ty Gwnn at which a former 2 I/C of a unit I served in was running. By this time I'd had other suicide attempts. Then other avenues were opened up to me. I got a call from Robin Short to attend a training session run by David Walters and then the lights came popping on all over the place. The time I did learning "The Walters method™" not only allowed me to get over my PTSD it also allowed me to use the other techniques I had learned to finally find freedom. I'm now sleeping through the night without any nightmares. I only take sleeping pills after a particularly hard day at work and I can actually remember having normal dreams.

Many PTSD casualties have been let down so many times they're afraid to go out of their comfort zone. They live in little cliques supporting each other, drinking, often taking drugs and letting out their aggression and misdirected anger. All I can say is give yourself permission to try it out. Give it a go. The training has certainly worked for me. I've had about dozen suppressed traumatic memories re-emerge since I did the training and I've dealt with them all using the techniques I've leaned. Even when I retold my PTSD story this time it wasn't that tough – I've had a major break through that I've never experienced before.

Doug Padgett, Cpl RAMC (Retd)

All this work has been conducted under the direct supervision of Dr Robin Short, the former Surgeon General of the British Army. Also we are working with a leading UK charity P3, *the social inclusion charity*, to create a social enterprise so this can be made available for all ex-servicemen suffering from PTSD.

In the next chapter Martin Kinsella will explain what the future holds for the casualties of PTSD and how P3 is spearheading a major charitable drive to provide the much needed relief our veterans need.

CHAPTER 10

MOVING FORWARDS

By
Martin Kinsella

The History

Between 2 April and 12 June 1982, 29,682 British personnel earned the South Atlantic Medal for service during the Falkland's war. Of these 255 died in combat. In 2002, a BBC report suggested that a greater number than those who gave their lives in the Falklands have since committed suicide. This report argued that the high number of suicides among Falklands veterans arose because of the failure to treat the mind "injury" known as Post Traumatic Stress Disorder (PTSD).

Current Casualties

Official US estimates suggest that some 15% of those who have seen combat service will suffer from PTSD over the long term. In the UK more conservative estimates are used which suggest that about 9% of combat veterans will suffer the long-term effects of PTSD. Drawing on these conservative estimates, as many as 2,600 Falklands veterans are likely to be long term PTSD casualties.

Individuals suffering from PTSD experience four main symptoms:

- intrusive memories
- sleep disturbance
- hyper arousal/avoidance behaviour
- emotional shutdown.

In extreme cases sufferers will commit suicide rather than continue to live with the effects of PTSD.

There is little support for these ex-services casualties. The NHS has acknowledged that it has not got the capacity to deal with the most severe cases, known as 'complex PTSD'. Meanwhile, one specialist charity, Combat Stress, which provides care to PTSD sufferers, saw a 26% increase in cases in 2006. The charity has stated that it is operating near to capacity.

Many PTSD casualties become alcohol and substance abusers, living in failed relationships or ending up on the street, where they become major users of the resources of night shelters, hostels, accident and emergency departments and the police. Even government figures confirm that studies have consistently found that between 20 and 25% of rough sleepers are ex-services personnel (Report on Rough Sleeping, Social Exclusion Unit, 1998). Figures from Crisis state that up to 30% of homeless people in hostels, day centres and soup runs have served in the forces (Lest We Forget: ex-servicemen and homelessness, Crisis, 2000). Crisis have found that the number of single homeless is in a range of between 310,000 and 380.000 and that around 25% of these are in hostels, B&B or in imminent threat of eviction (How Many, How Much?, Crisis, 2003). These figures confirm that there is significant unmet need amongst our ex-service personnel, this is of course compounded by the upwards of 24,000 people who leave the forces each year.

The Royal British Legion and the Soldiers, Sailors, Airmen and Families Association jointly run a prison in-reach service to support veterans who are incarcerated. According to the National Ex-Serviceman's Association as many as 7% of the prison population (over 5,000 inmates) are ex-servicemen. Many find themselves in prison as a direct result of their actions (violence, manslaughter and even murder) which can be linked to untreated PTSD.

Many PTSD casualties make extraordinary efforts to avoid triggering the extreme adverse responses associated with the condition. Unfortunately, because of the attendant media coverage, avoiding the 25th anniversary commemorations of the Falklands campaign will prove nearly impossible. Worse, many veterans will discover that, though the planned commemorations will trigger their PTSD, little or no effective support will be made available to help them deal with their condition and its associated problems.

The Plan

Until now there has been no widely available, effective support for PTSD casualties. However, a group of private, public and voluntary sector bodies is setting out to change this. This collaborative effort will involve the award winning charity P3 *the social inclusion charity*, Help Me Overcome (a company specialising in protecting orgaisations from the liability and loss associated with workplace stress and PTSD resulting from accidents and natural disasters) and other ex-services organisations.

Help Me Overcome has developed a trauma recovery protocol which appears to be highly effective in overcoming the various problems associated with PTSD. P3, *the social inclusion charity*, has volunteered to use its best endeavours to quickly develop PTSD support services for Falklands veterans who need help.

The service will be outcomes focused, in that it will be developed and designed to achieve positive results for the people that use it, this being both the starting point in the service design and the end point in its delivery. The service will be overseen by a Consultant Clinical Psychologist and Registered Mental Health Nurses; furthermore all staff taking part will be trained and experienced. The service will also incorporate a practical level of support for service users who need support and assistance in accessing training, accommodation or seeking employment.

P3 will commission a major university research department to undertake an observational study of the programme in order to learn lessons and consolidate the learning from this initiative for wider use and dissemination.

The collaboration will be conducted under the guidance of an advisory board led by Major General Robin Short CB MBChB FRCS (Glas) Surgeon General British Army (retired), and former Director General, British Army Medical Services.

Delivery

It must be stated that in order to take this project forward we need to raise a significant amount of money, around £500,000 to run the service for a year including start up costs and research costs. The service in this time will have capacity for around 300 service users.

Given that we achieve this and the outcomes are favourable, we will then seek funding for a PTSD outreach campaign to be rolled out from 2007 onwards, the aim being to provide the recovery protocol to any Falklands veteran who is suffering from PTSD and requests support. The objective is to make support available for up to 2,000 veterans who may need this service. Based on funding estimates provided by P3, the delivery cost for each casualty can be expected to be in excess of £1,500.

To make this programme a success, we need to raise a minimum of £2,000,000 by the end of 2007 to meet predicted demand from British Falklands veterans alone.

It doesn't end there

Once the initial fund-raising campaign and training programme has been completed, there will be ongoing value to our civilian and military society. As a result of this programme the PTSD intervention method will have been independently observed by leading academics and the programme will be further refined.

An established team of trained and experienced counsellors will then be available to provide this service to other groups in our society. The model will also be offered more widely, for example, for use in treating both complex and acute/chronic PTSD (such as sexual abuse, domestic violence, rape trauma, industrial accidents and civil disasters) and to the MoD to provide preventative support and intervention to current service personnel as well as Iran and Afghanistan campaign veterans.

The mission statement of P3 is:

P3 exists to operate services and create opportunities for vulnerable and disadvantaged people that offer effective and lasting routes out of social exclusion and homelessness.

All funds raised by P3 from the sale of this book will be designated specifically for the purpose of developing and providing PTSD services.

Please visit www.p3charity.com/ONCEisENOUGH to make a donation.

We thank you for your support.

ABOUT THE AUTHOR

David Walters left Bolton School in 1980 to join Britannia Royal Naval College prior to his training at the Royal Naval Engineering College, Manadon. He qualified as a Weapons Engineer Officer in the Royal Navy Submarine Service serving in both nuclear hunter killer submarines and diesel electric boats. After a brief period in the Canadian submarine service he entered civilian employment as an emergency management consultant.

David gained extensive experience working in the nuclear power industry in North America as an emergency management and security consultant. During this period he served on the Disaster Management Council of the American Society of Industrial Security and was a regular participant at the Ontario based World Conference on Disaster Management. Post 9/11 David delivered a series of lectures on building life safety planning in New York, Washington DC, Chicago and Toronto.

It was his work with multinational corporations as a crisis management consultant that caused him to develop a keen interest in the effect of operational stress on first responders. This resulted in researching many methods for overcoming stress which led him to develop a technique known as "The Walters Method™" for teaching people to become resilient to stress. That is learning how to avoid becoming stressed rather than simply attempting to manage stress. A variant of this method was developed in response to the plight of British service personnel returning from Afghanistan and Iraq, which has been used to good effect in teaching veterans who to overcome their symptoms of PTSD. David now leads Help Me Overcome (www.helpmeovercome.com) a growing company specialising in the area of corporate and executive stress resilience and Post Traumatic Stress Disorder.

In his younger days, David was a keen mountaineer and caver, but his passion of curry cookery and real ale has put paid to those more adventurous pursuits. David is happily married to Yve and lives in Lincolnshire with his teenage son and daughter.

ONCE is enough!

Help veterans to stop reliving traumatic experiences

For twenty five years Steve "Taff" Horvath hasn't slept a single night without having a nightmare. Night after night he ends up patrolling grounds, searching for an enemy. Vivid and horrific images constantly flash through his mind. And it's not just the night. Flashbacks, major outbursts of anger, fear, paranoia are all symptoms common not just to Taff but to thousands of Soldiers, Sailors and Airmen suffering from Post Traumatic Stress Disorder (PTSD). Daily trauma, violence and fear for both them and their families.

Little effective support has been available – until now. **With your help we can provide the specialist care that Taff and his family need.**

This year Taff was able to overcome his nightmare. He said, "I don't know how this programme works. I don't care. All I know is that I am symptom free".

But today over 2,000 families like Taff's still have no access to effective means of support. Your gift, whatever you can afford, will help one family live symptom free for the first time in years.

Please be generous and help those who relive the horrors of war every day end the nightmare of PTSD.

Please turn over to find out how you can help...

ONCE is enough

Here's my gift to help one family

First Name: ....

Family Name: ....

Address: ....

....

Postcode: ....

Email: ....

Tel: ....

Please use my gift where it is most needed to help one person become sympton free: (Please make cheques payable to 'P3')

→ £1,000 will cover the cost of a three day residential course

→ £50 will fund an initial assessment of need

→ £?? All contributions are welcome and will be used for PTSD services

→ £500 will provide follow up support after the residential programme

→ £1,500 will provide a residential programme with follow up support

Gift Aid It *giftaid it*

Signing this declaration will allow P3 to reclaim the tax you pay on your donations at no cost to you. It will increase the value of your gift by 28%.

I would like P3 to treat all my donations as gift aid donations until I notify you otherwise.

Signed: Date:
....

Registered Charity No 703163. A company limited by guarantee

Please send your gift to:

P3, Gladstone House, Market Street, Ilkeston, Derbyshire, DE7 5RB

Or give online at www.p3charity.org/ONCEisENOUGH

Give now: www.p3charity.com/ONCEisENOUGH

Printed in the United Kingdom
by Lightning Source UK Ltd.
124328UK00001BA/49/A